THE GAME CHANGERS

Women Entrepreneurs Redefining the Rules

KIRAN MANRAL

Om **Books** International

First published in 2025 by

Om Books International

Corporate & Editorial Office
A-12, Sector 64, Noida 201 301
Uttar Pradesh, India
Phone: +91 120 477 4100
Email: editorial@ombooks.com
Website: www.ombooksinternational.com

Sales Office
107, Ansari Road, Darya Ganj,
New Delhi 110 002, India
Phone: +91 11 4000 9000
Email: sales@ombooks.com
Website: www.ombooks.com

ISBN: 978-93-6395-457-1

Printed in India

10 9 8 7 6 5 4 3 2 1

Kiran Manral is an award-winning and bestselling author, TEDx speaker, columnist and feminist. A prolific writer, she has authored books across genres in both fiction and non-fiction.

Kiran Manral debuted as a novelist in 2011 with *The Reluctant Detective*. Since then, she has authored many books in fiction across subgenres like romance and chick lit (*Once Upon A Crush*, 2014; *All Aboard*, 2015; *Saving Maya*, 2017); horror (*The Face at the Window*, 2016; *More Things in Heaven and Earth*, 2021); psychological thriller (*Missing, Presumed Dead*, 2018); science fiction (*All Those Who Wander*, 2023); dark fantasy (*The Moon in the Lining of Her Skin*, 2024); comic mystery (*The Reluctant Detective*, 2011 and *The Kitty Party Murder*, 2020). In non-fiction, her work includes *Karmic Kids* (2015), *A Boy's Guide to Growing Up* (2016), *True Love Stories* (2017), *13 Steps to Bloody Good Parenting* (2019), *Raising Children with Hope and Wonder in Times of a Pandemic and Climate Change* (2020), *Rising: 30 Women Who Changed India* (2022) and *Rising 2.0: 20 More Women Who Changed India* (2024).

Her short stories have appeared in magazines like *Verve* and *Cosmopolitan* on the Juggernaut app and in anthologies like *Chicken Soup for the Soul, Have a Safe Journey* (2017), *Boo* (2017), *The Best Asian Speculative Fiction* (2018), *City of Screams* (2019), *The Hachette Book of Indian Detective Fiction* (2024) and *Hell Hath No Fury* (2024).

Her articles and columns have appeared in *The Times of India, Tehelka, DNA, Yowoto, Shethepeople, DailyO, Scroll, Buzzfeed, New Woman, Femina, Verve, Elle, Cosmopolitan, Conde Nast Traveller, DB Post, The Telegraph, The Asian Age, iDiva, People, Sakal Times* and more. *The Sunday Guardian* named her book *Karmic Kids: The Story of Parenting Nobody Told You* one of the best five parenting books written by Indian authors in 2015. One review called her the "Bombeck of Bombay".

The Face at the Window was highly praised by critics and included in BuzzingBubs' list of must-read books by contemporary women authors as well as The Ladies Finger's selection of the top 30 books written by women authors in 2016. Kiran may have very well pioneered the "Himalayan Gothic" genre with this work, according to the *Times of India*. HoneyKids Asia listed *The Face at the Window,* along with international bestsellers like *Ring,* among its top picks for Asian horror books. *DesiBlitz* named her among "top seven horror writers from India".

She was included in *Monster Complex's* global/genre lists such as Urban Fantasy Showcase: 100 Authors to Know and Asian/Pacific horror authors.

An ex-journalist, qualitative market researcher and trendspotter, Kiran was a mentor with Vital Voices Global Mentoring Walk. The Indian Council of UN Relations (ICUNR) supported by the Ministry for Women and Child Development, Government of India, awarded her the International Women's Day Award 2018 for excellence in the field of writing. Her novella, *Saving Maya,* was longlisted for the 2018 Saboteur Awards, UK, supported by the Arts Council England. In 2021, she was named in the Womennovator 1000 Women of Asia list.

The Red Dot Foundation and Beyond Black, in partnership with the Office of the Principal Scientific Advisor, Government of India, and British High Commission, New Delhi, named her one of the 75 Iconic Indian women in STEAM (fields of science, technology, engineering, arts and mathematics) in 2022.

In addition, she served as Sheroes' mentor, an advisor on the Board of Literature Studio, Delhi, and a member of the Kumaon Literary Festival planning board. She co-curated Women Writer's Fest by SheThePeople.TV and co-curated Festivelle 2016.

She has spoken and participated in panels at India's major literary festivals, including the Hindu Lit Fest, the Jaipur Lit Fest, the Times Lit Fest (Kolkata, Delhi, Bengaluru), the Matrubhumi Lit Fest, the Bangalore Lit Fest, the Kala Ghoda Arts Festival, the Brahmaputra Lit Fest (Guwahati), the Kumaon Lit Fest (Nainital), the Dehradun Lit Fest, the Ahmedabad Lit Fest and the Pune International Lit Fest. She has also spoken at esteemed conferences, including FICCI Frames 2018 and the Bangalore Tech Summit 2017, as well as at educational institutions like IIT Bhubaneswar; IIT Roorkee; IIT Madras; IIMA; NMIMS; Mithibai College; St Xavier's College, Mumbai; Vaze College, Mumbai; Vibgyor High School, Mumbai; and NM College. She has a formidable reputation as a social media influencer.

She was part of the core founding team that ran the initiatives like Child Sexual Abuse Awareness Month and Violence Against Women Awareness Month for four years. She also initiated India Helps, a volunteer network that assisted 26/11 attack victims with their recovery.

After earning a degree in English literature from Mithibai College in Mumbai, she briefly worked in the advertising industry before transitioning to journalism with publications like the *Dalal Street Investment Journal, The Asian Age, The Times of India* and *Cosmopolitan.*

She then went on to start her own business with Soul Communications, a web content supplying company and then Karma Communications, a full-service advertising agency. She returned to the formal workforce as India culture lead and trendspotter at Gartner Iconoculture, US, and then as senior consultant Vector Insights and consultant ideas editor, SheThePeople.TV. She is also the co-host of the popular podcast *Not Your Aunty*.

Kiran and her family reside in Mumbai. You may contact her on Instagram at @kiranmanral and on X.

*To my eight-year-old self who opened a library at home
complete with proper ledgers, shelves and late-fee charges.
To my 12-year-old self who filled out forms, obtained
subscribers for international pen pals, posted and undertook
other tasks for a charge.
To my 14-year-old self who bought T-shirts from a fashion
street and resold them in class.
This book is a nudge to myself.*

Contents

Introduction

There is freedom waiting for you,
On the breezes of the sky,
And you ask 'What if I fall?'
Oh but my darling,
What if you fly?

— Erin Hanson

I have always believed in stories. I have always believed that the stories we tell ourselves shape the stories we will believe about ourselves. I think that there aren't enough stories about women being told and that they have not been told enough. This was a gap I set out to fill with my previous books on Indian women who shaped their worlds with quiet courage, fierce conviction and an unwillingness to accept the limits society imposed upon them.

The Game Changers is a continuation of that effort to chronicle remarkable achievements of women, but with a significantly different lens. This book trains the spotlight on 14 exceptional women who have not just broken barriers but have built entirely new landscapes.

These are women who transformed ideas into enterprises, setbacks into stepping stones and stereotypes into shattered ceilings. They sometimes failed, but that did not deter them from trying again. And again. And at times, yet again. In this book, we celebrate these achievers who not only dared to dream, create enterprises and companies, but also communities and conversations that are changing the face of entrepreneurship in India.

In this book, you will meet Anu Acharya, whose pioneering work in genomics is making healthcare more predictive and personalized in India. Ameera Shah, who turned a single family-run pathology lab into one of the most respected diagnostic networks in the country. Ridhi Dongursee, who is playing a key role in fostering more thoughtful investing practices among Indian women and boosting their confidence in money management.

We have Rashi Sanon Narang who tapped into the underappreciated world of pet care to build a thriving brand that treats pets like family, and Namrata Asthana, who along with her partners, has created a quiet revolution in the way a nation of tea drinkers now looks at coffee. Ayushi Gudwani stands out for creating intelligent fashion, which uses technology and data to customize apparel to real bodies and requirements.

You will read about Rachana Gupta who co-founded a tech platform offering ayurveda-based remedies for women's gynaecological issues, which has now gone offline; Aditi Gupta, who has transformed menstrual education in India by breaking taboos one comic strip at a time, and former IAF officer Neelu Khatri, with an impeccable track record in the defence and aerospace industry, championing both innovation and inclusion, currently managing India's latest entrant into the domestic aviation space, which she co-founded.

Apurva Purohit brings in the voice of a corporate veteran, author and mentor whose leadership has inspired countless women to step into boardrooms with confidence, and who is now focused on empowering rural women. Sisters Taniya and Sujata Biswas demonstrate how innovation and technology can coexist harmoniously through their reimagination of the way a sari is worn. Then there is Vineeta Singh whose difficult journey to becoming a beauty mogul is characterized by persistence and extremely bold choices, including turning down a lucrative job offer, to get straight into entrepreneurship. And last but not the least, Naiyya Saggi whose ground-breaking work in femtech and parent-tech has revolutionized how Indian parents access knowledge, healthcare and community.

Each of the woman featured here did more than just build a business—they spotted problems and turned them into opportunities for growth. They disrupted, they designed, they led from the front, and often, with their hearts.

The Game Changers is far from being just a business book. It is a tribute to the fire that fuels women who rise, over and over again, to create, lead and leave a lasting legacy. All of them embody the entrepreneurial spirit that is both unique and individualistic.

This is not just a collection of their success stories—it is their stories, in their words. It is a chronicle of decisions, some risky, some radical, often rebellious; of leaps of faith and the quiet, relentless work that follows; of the failures from which they recovered, undaunted; of building with intention and leading with empathy. These trailblazers remind us that entrepreneurship involves more than just making money or providing goods or services—it is about purpose.

May their stories inspire yours. May these enable you to trust your voice and your vision.

1

"I am extremely proud about having changed the conversation around menstruation and enabling people to think about it in a positive way"

Aditi Gupta
Co-Founder and Managing Partner,
Menstrupedia

At the age of 12, Aditi Gupta from Garwaha, Jharkhand, had her first period. Nothing out of the ordinary here, girls all around the world begin menstruating at about that age, so did Aditi. After all, wasn't it part and parcel of growing up, of becoming a woman?

However, little did Aditi know about what menstruation entailed—there was no healthy conversation around it at home, neither by her mother, nor her aunts. The only thing she knew is that a period came with restrictions. She was forbidden from entering the kitchen and the temple, told not to sit on the bed else the bedding would need to be changed, all the restrictions imposed by tradition and superstition because a menstruating woman was considered impure. Even sanitary napkins were out of reach to her because it was embarrassing to go to the medical store to buy a packet. She had to make do with homemade cloths.

She would only learn about menstruation a few years later. It would not be until she shifted to a hostel in another city that she would buy herself the very first pack of sanitary napkins because her roommates were using them and she could easily buy the napkins at the stores with them.

That young Aditi would grow up to establish Menstrupedia—a fast-growing start-up that offers high social impact educational materials in the form of comic books, workshops and animated videos—to teach young girls about menstruation. It came about quite serendipitously, as most good things do. Aditi eventually moved away from Garwaha, thanks to her parents who had more ambition for her than stultifying in the small town.

She went on to become an engineering graduate, and joined the National Institute of Design (NID), Gandhinagar, which was life-changing for her in more ways than one. This was where she would meet, fall in love and eventually marry her batchmate, Tuhin Paul. And it was at the NID, where the idea of Menstrupedia was first sown in her mind.

Drawing upon her experience of dealing with the trauma of menstruation, Aditi began exploring it as a subject for her final-year project, with Tuhin as the partner of the project. She researched the subject for over a year as a Ford Foundation research scholar, speaking with gynaecologists and girls, before creating the comic book which had a doctor and three young girls as the main characters. The idea of the *Menstrupedia Comic*, a must-read period guide for every nine-year-old girl, was revolutionary in itself. It took them some time to formalize it.

After having worked for three years in the e-learning industry, the couple decided to take a leap of faith and start Menstrupedia as a social initiative. They also got married to each other at this time. They founded it in 2012 and a year later they were joined by Rajat Mittal, a graduate from Dhirubhai Ambani Institute of Information and Communication Technology (DA-IICT) and a postgraduate in computer science from Arizona State University. Tuhin and Aditi used their savings for the initial investment. Quitting their jobs and letting go of a steady income was a risk they were willing to take because it was something they had to do, something that was important to Aditi, and now to Tuhin as well.

From a final-year project, that comic book has grown to become an online platform that provides friendly and informed advice and information on puberty and sexuality for pre-teens and teenagers. On the website, you can find comic books, blogs, Q&A and a section to learn. Menstrupedia's comic book is available in all Indian languages, and is also printed in 11 other countries in their local languages. Aditi wrote the first Menstrupedia comic book, and Tuhin illustrated it. They themselves made the initial materials now used in schools across India to teach young girls about menstruation and has also worked on collaborative campaigns with brands to dispel myths about menstruation. Menstrupedia has made a difference in the lives of 15 million girls, and more than 36 schools in India use the various comic books as a part of their curriculum. Melinda Gates had this to say about the comic book, "This is a great creative solution to a tough cultural challenge."

Aditi even made it to the Forbes India 30 under 30 list in 2014. What were the odds of a girl from the small town of Garwaha making it to the Forbes India 30 under 30? Next to none. But here she was, bringing pride to her hometown.

The comic book has been used by many NGOs and even monasteries in remote places like Ladakh to introduce young girls to the concept of menstruation and the bodily changes they will undergo, as well as to dispel myths and superstitions around periods. It wasn't easy, they didn't expect it to be. Working full time on the initiative, managing funds was a major challenge for them. However, they managed to sustain on their savings for only a year despite functioning on a shoestring budget.

Convincing investors was a hard task. They would come up against a wall the moment they said they wanted to create an educational tool related to menstruation. They launched a crowd-funding campaign when they had only two months of run time on their current funds. They had even moved to a tiny one-room flat to cut their own monthly expenses, but they found love and support from people who sent them far more money than what they had expected.

In the year 2022, the innovators got to pitch their educational app, website and comic book, which aim to change the narrative around periods, in the first season of the popular show *Shark Tank*. It was an unnerving experience but one that catapulted Menstrupedia and Aditi into the spotlight. They found an investor in Namita Thapar who decided to invest in Menstrupedia in exchange for 10 per cent equity.

Menstrupedia offers comic books for girls as well as boys, battling puberty and related issues. They even conduct workshops and masterclasses on these subjects. Aditi hopes that her efforts will be instrumental in having the next generation of Indian girls grow up without the shame that previous generations, including hers, have associated with menstruation.

Here are the excerpts from our interview in 2023 and updated later:

How did a girl from Jharkhand become a fierce advocate for menstrual awareness? Tell us about your earliest recollections and the experience of dealing with menstruation as a child. I believe you could not even buy sanitary napkins. How did that impact you? What I do and why I do have a lot to do with how I battled period taboos as a young girl growing up in Jharkhand.

I was in the seventh grade when I first got my period. I had met with a serious accident before that. I had a severe injury to my head and a part of my skull had to be cut. I had to undergo a major surgery during which they put a catheter in my urethra for urination. When they removed the catheter perhaps my urethra must have gotten hurt and I began bleeding. I was completely bedridden. At this point, my mother thought that I was starting my period. This was when she decided to tell me about menstruation. I clearly remember our chat. This is what she said, 'You know sometimes when your cousins tell you that they cannot go to a temple or oil their hair, this is what happens. You bleed down there for five to six days. I also got my period when I was around your age.'

There were no names given to the body parts or any explanations offered about the changes the body undergoes. She simply spelled out the rules I had to follow on those days. She made it sound like menstruation was something dirty or impure.

That conversation made me anxious about menstruation. This was in Ranchi. My parents had taken me to RMCH Ranchi for my surgery.

I did start my period after a few months of returning from Ranchi. You can say, I was kind of prepared for it.

My mother bathed me with two-and-a-half lotas of water to reduce the duration of my menstruation. Apparently, this was a common ritual. Since she used to bleed heavily, this was her way to help her child. Later, I found a lack of awareness about menstruation even among erudite people—so my highly educated parents were not an exception. My mother tried to ensure that I committed no 'sin' on those days. And I did not have access to sanitary napkins, actually none of the women had access, because we could not go and buy them, it was not the done thing. The question wasn't whether we wanted to buy them or not.

My parents have moved mountains to put me where I am today. I grew up in an extremely backward place where girls were married off at a very early age and dowry deaths were common. Ma and Baba put everything at stake as far as my education was concerned. My father sold our huge house and moved to Ranchi only to provide me with a better education. He couldn't put me in a hostel when I was young because of my surgery. Hence, their attitude towards periods baffles me even today. But I remember I was not allowed to ride the bicycle to my school or tuition classes and my father would drop me on his scooter on those days. Ma and I would use rags, wash them and dry them in the sun. When you wash the cloth that is soaked in menstrual blood and reuse it, it becomes coarse after two-three cycles. It used to give me rashes. The rainy season would make it worse as these cloths would not dry and there would be a foul smell also.

How did you decide to make spreading information about menstruation and dispelling myths surrounding it your life's mission?

At NID, we had to pick up a four-week project during my postgraduation. It was imperative to select one that was related to some social problem. As a communications design student, I was fascinated with how people, especially kids, learn. And you always tend to circle back to yourself because once you understand yourself and your problems better, you understand the world better.

This also has to do a lot with Tuhin and my love story. Since we were batchmates, we used to do a lot of projects together, and eventually we fell in love. I am an extremely hardworking person, but during my period, I would not be as active. I would tell my boyfriend what I was going through. It was difficult for me to speak with any male about this, and he was the first man I had spoken with about my period. I would discuss in detail my menstrual cramps and mood swings with him.

Tuhin hailed from a family where they were two brothers, and his mother never told them about periods. And in school, his biology teacher skipped the chapter on menstruation.

So here we were, two 24-year-olds with no clue about periods! It was around this time that I began reading up and realized that periods were also called menstruation, which was very different from mensuration. I felt, really, what was this happening inside me?

As we began talking about it to our batchmates, we realized it was not an easy conversation to have. However, we were not the first ones discussing a taboo topic on campus. There was a senior of ours who did a project on the usage of condoms. I think NID is a place where you get to meet people who would not feel shy or embarrassed about discussing such issues. This was way back in in 2008, things were very different back then and exposure to media was limited.

Thankfully, when I submitted my proposal, my teachers encouraged me to do this project. That was really the beginning of Menstrupedia and how we started. I was an engineer, and I led a very independent life away from home. However, before my conversations about periods with Tuhin, I had never looked up for information on menstruation. This was unacceptable behaviour for any decent girl. The shame was that deep-rooted.

Tuhin and I saw it more as a communication design problem. We studied a lot of complex concepts at NID, but this was a simple concept of how the egg is released and how it is travelling. But we had never studied it in school, and we did not know exactly how this process happens in the female body. If you go to a classroom, there would be a diagram of the digestive system, the respiratory system but not the reproductive system.

Why? Because it was related to private body parts? Nobody told us where the uterus was located. All we knew was that we would bleed, but from where? It was all very vague.

As we started talking to our batchmates, we realized that everyone had a unique story to tell and the taboo was so common that it didn't matter what culture you were from.

Then we began our investigation by visiting schools in Gandhinagar and going through textbooks and found that nothing much had changed. People were unwilling and unable to talk about it, and that was what we needed to change. This reinforced our belief that this was a communication design problem.

Initially, the idea was to first successfully complete this four-week project. The environment in NID allows these kinds of projects to flourish, the professors there help you question societal norms and provide you with the tools to do so. We were taught about society, technology, human psychology, metaphors, human emotions and how these things combine to help you design solutions better. I still fondly remember my guide Gayatri Menon, who was the first teacher who ever believed in me.

Tell us about how you happened to go to National Institute of Design and how your years there impacted you?

Since I went through these two major surgeries, the first in standard seven and the second in standard nine, I was never a teacher's pet because I was always lagging behind in my studies. I think most of my childhood went in these surgeries—going through one, prepping for the other, then recovery. Understandably, my parents were extremely protective of me because I was leading a fragile life. I was failing in school, but I think it was the Indian education system that failed me terribly.

At my core, I feel that I am an educator more than anything else. My grades at the engineering college were so low that I could not even go for the campus placements except for one. I had scored only 58 per cent marks altogether. Thankfully, I got an offer from a company but it was in Delhi and I didn't want to go there as that place felt very unsafe to me as a girl. I had been groped and harassed, as it was with most girls, in Agra. I had somehow felt that Delhi was not going to be any different.

When I was in the fourth year of engineering, one of my seniors got through NID. So I, along with two of my batchmates, applied there, and engineering design was the obvious and natural choice. That was my only reason for applying to NID.

I did not know that NID was going to be so great. For the first time, I enjoyed giving a test so much. You know why?

In the entrance test, I was asked to write down my thoughts rather than create diagrams. Where do they do that? Up until now, I was only required to perform calculations, create diagrams and other similar tasks.

That world felt extremely complex to me when compared to this world that encouraged me to think creatively and express myself. For the first time at NID I felt that learning was so much fun that I stuck to seeing things the way I wanted to see them. Education was making me use my learnings and put it to practical use. Whatever we were learning, whether it be films, communications, ethnography, social mores, representation in media and films, I could put it to use in communication tools. I learnt that a story could be used to teach certain things and bring about change in the lives of people.

Even though I was terrified of my professor, Gayatri Menon, at that time, she really pushed me in the right direction. She served as my mentor. She made me watch *Father, Son, and Holy War* by Anand Patwardhan and read *The Naked Woman* by Desmond Morris, amongst others.

My views on women's bodies, the politics surrounding them and feminism were all shaped by these novels and movies. I realized that I had been viewing the world from a very different perspective. And made me raise many questions like why menstruation is viewed in such a dirty manner.

Given how popular pornography is, why doesn't it educate people about periods? Porn artists don't get periods at all one would think.

Tuhin used to do a lot of animation in his engineering days. He was a fierce advocate of storytelling through animation. At NID, he was learning how one could use storytelling in communication design to communicate complex concepts to people.

The use of narrative to convey forbidden and complicated ideas to conservative societies, such as child sexual abuse or domestic violence, captivated him. Since storytelling was becoming a really powerful tool to bring about social change, we decided to follow suit and teach people about periods via a comic book. Thus, studying at NID became one of the turning points of my life. That was where I discovered that teaching others about menstruation was my calling.

Your husband and co-founder of Menstrupedia, Tuhin, was also your batchmate at NID. Share some anecdotes about how you got together as a couple?

Tuhin and I worked on projects together, talked about what to do, and had dreams about what we wanted to become, and what we saw ourselves becoming. Our friendship and love revolved around this.

We were a great team at college. Tuhin was an A+ through and through, whereas I was a C- in my first semester and eventually became an A+. I think his grade fluctuated when we fell in love as we weren't really studying much.

We always wanted to do our own thing. Menstrupedia has a lot to do with our goals.

Tuhin was always a dreamer. He would never get scared of dreaming big, and he taught me to dream big too.

I was always good with my research, and I loved talking to people. And Tuhin was a very skilled person. So, I would come and share all my data and observations and learnings with him, and he would figure out how to use it. So, it was a very yin-yang kind of relationship, which is the way it is even today. I am glad things worked out the way they have. I am thrilled that our one idea changed the lives of so many girls.

The Indian youths nowadays are incredible—just look at the kind of money they are handling and the companies they are setting up. But somehow kids in the age group of nine to 14 are finding it difficult to flourish as they think that their parents don't understand them and parents think that their kids are not listening to them. So a major part of our work is to listen to parents who have adolescent kids because there is so much potential in this age group which we as a society or even at the family level are not harnessing. This is why we have decided to educate both girls and families about menstruation.

How did Menstrupedia evolve from the subject of your thesis at NID to its current form? Did you face any resistance from your family when you decided to become a social entrepreneur?

Thanks to my engineering background, I turned this four-semester project into a game. When I presented my work to the jury comprising professors they were keen to know about my learnings from the project. The question *'Apney kya kiya?'* was thrown my way. I had to evaluate myself.

I was asked how I was going to distribute the game. How will girls play the game on their computers? This was way before 4G. This was in 2008–09 so forget about the internet, even regular and steady supply of electricity was a problem. So making anything computer-based seemed like an exclusive media accessible to only a few of the people, not everyone. And that is why we went ahead with print media because it is not dependent on electricity, the internet or accessibility.

A comic book had a strong market fit. Anybody who can read can easily learn about periods because there are many pictures and the dialogues and sentences are short and in simple language.

As our final assignment, we were expected to complete a six-month-long internship at NID. I applied to the Ford Foundation, which funded projects related to girls' education. I got the scholarship and I made it my thesis project.

Tuhin thought of the name, we started Menstrupedia after we were married and while working in different firms in Mumbai.

We were creating learning tools to teach kids and grown-ups different concepts. Although we were both learning how to use our tools on a large scale, we always wanted to work independently and return to Ahmedabad as we anticipated a low burn rate there. We had planned to quit our jobs and devote ourselves full time to develop our idea, but we were not even sure what it was, and whether we would stick with only the menstruation idea.

When we finally left our jobs, our parents felt cheated because they had invested a lot in our education and had high hopes for our comfortable career. It was their dream to see us make it big in life. Our parents made a concerted effort to convince us that we need not quit our jobs to pursue our dreams because periods were not a trending topic then, neither was entrepreneurship. And Make in India has gained popularity only recently. In our hometown, parents would open a cycle repair shop or a vegetable stall for their wards if they did not do well in studies or land a decent job. It was all the more challenging for us, since we are both the eldest children of our parents.

We are very close to our parents and we are held up as role models to our younger siblings so for us to quit our jobs was quite a shock to them. Also, we failed to share our plans with them properly, which added to their anxiety levels. They simply couldn't understand how people with such high incomes could leave their jobs to create a comic that would educate girls about periods.

This rancour between our parents and us must have lasted for a year or so. However, parents being parents, they eventually came around. As our product started selling, and Menstrupedia gained more recognition and success and became self-sustaining, they warmed up to the idea.

Raising funds was another big challenge that we faced. Initially, when Tuhin and I were pitching our ideas, it was difficult for him to speak about periods because the stereotyping was so strong. He was once asked, 'Do you have the agency to talk about menstruation?' That was when we decided that I will be the one who would talk about periods. After that, he would take over and not much has changed.

Tuhin is the magician who handles everything backstage while I am the one who speaks about everything in front of the audience. In 2012, we got selected for the initial round of the Economic Times Power of Ideas—the entrepreneurship initiative was launched in 2009 during the economic slowdown. Again, all of these things were very new— incubation programmes, start-up ecosystem were just getting started.

I don't want to offend the four middle-aged men who were on the jury, but they were shockingly clueless about periods. One of the jury members even went ahead and declared, 'We will read up about menstruation on Wikipedia.'

The issue is so obscure that you are not aware of its magnitude, and the size of the problem is the size of the market that you can capture, and the size of the problem you can solve. We did not make it to the final round. I recall how devastated we were when we returned to our friend's place that day. This rejection only reinforced our determination to make this idea work, because when you have leading investors of the country not understanding the magnitude of the problem, it definitely had to be addressed.

There was a lot of scope to educate these men, but our focus and expertise was always with kids and our tools were designed to teach only them. Thankfully, we got a lot of free press and good PR, which really helped us in crowdfunding. We only aimed to raise a total of four lakh rupees, but we ended up raising 5.5 lakh rupees. And this was back when crowdfunding was not very common and people were hesitant in transferring funds online.

So, we raised this money for printing the first 1,000 copies. And in 2022, we raised a lot more money with the entrepreneur and angel investor Namita Thapar at *Shark Tank*.

At any point, did you come up against biases, invisible or otherwise, when speaking with venture capitalists (VCs) or investors as a woman? How did you deal with it?

Interestingly, the biases benefitted me a lot. For example, women entrepreneurs should not be a separate category but wherever that category is I always feature in the top 10. When it comes to earning money though, I am nowhere near the top 10.

However, I always made it to the lists of the people who have challenged social norms or successful women entrepreneurs from small towns. The tag of a 'female entrepreneur' works for a small bootstrapped company like ours, as we don't have big budgets for marketing and promotion. For instance, we can't do ads in *Femina* by paying lakhs of rupees but when it writes a feature about successful women social entrepreneurs and includes me, the publicity of our work is taken care of.

So, being a woman entrepreneur has helped me thus far. When it comes to VCs and investors, it has a lot to do with the kind of business we are. Our business model is what is more important rather than my gender. Even if female entrepreneurship is associated with tokenism, I have met many women entrepreneurs in India who are fiercely passionate about uplifting other women.

I like to see the bright side of things; I must encourage rather than merely criticize. Namita has been very supportive. You see, even in the *Shark Tank* episode, we were to dilute 20 per cent but eventually we diluted only 10 per cent of our company. Her team has been very supportive, and we have been transparent with them about our monthly growth, sales matrix and other related things. I have never experienced discrimination. Instead, being a woman has always worked to my advantage.

Tell us about your* Shark Tank *experience, the funding received and how it has helped you scale up. What is your revenue model now, and how do you plan to reach sustainability?
Absolutely perfect, and a very positive experience. We had done only one or two fundraising attempts before *Shark Tank* and everywhere we

were harassed. People were insensitive about the idea. We had never attempted to raise funds until we had a solid business model. I think the *Shark Tank* experience was really beneficial, and it is one of the most beautiful things that the Indian start-up ecosystem has to offer at the moment.

The entire team has been extremely encouraging. The final pitch that the audience sees on television is actually the result of a great deal of effort on the part of the team. Take a look at how strong the entire *Shark Tank* team is, how they source applications, how they find project ideas from across the country, how the auditions are conducted, how they train people to talk in a certain way, how they teach business terms to entrepreneurs, how they prepare people to present their ideas.

Although the contestants are talented and hardworking, not all of them are adept in presenting their ideas in a way that is both attention-grabbing and understandable to the general public. You only spend just an hour with the Sharks, and while they are lowering the stakes and investing real money in companies, there will always be drama. But their larger goal is to invest in ideas and companies that they believe have potential.

The Indian market has a lot of potential, and it is amazing how the market is growing, how many people we have in the nation, how much we can consume, how our purchasing power has increased over the past decade and how much we are investing in women's health compared with a decade ago. We had an incredible experience of being on the first season of *Shark Tank.*

What have been your learnings from entrepreneurship?

If there is one thing I have learnt it is, to quote Maya Angelou, 'Each time a woman stands up for herself, without knowing it possibly, without claiming it, she stands up for all women.' This is something I have personally witnessed. We created the comic book to teach nine-year-old Aditi growing up in Garwaha. Her parents couldn't teach her; her teachers couldn't teach her either. The lessons learned include the fact that India is a huge market and that you should try to address any issues that are bothering you for yourself first. If it works for you, it will work for thousands of others, and 10 people will be eager to pay you for your services.

What would you tell any woman looking to become an entrepreneur?

It is a marathon, a lifestyle choice that you make, and ultimately, you must put in the hours and the effort. It was a magical journey for us as parents too because we could bring our kid to the office, we designed our office like that. I wouldn't do anything differently, perhaps have my first child earlier than I did. Perhaps I grew a little more mature after I had my first child, we became very goal-oriented people and began to pursue goals very seriously and methodically.

This can be a politically incorrect statement but having a kid truly broadens your view on life, and then becoming a mother makes you so much fierce and fearless. I am not saying that a woman has to become a mother to be fearless, not at all, but just that becoming a mother is another level of badassery for a woman completely. I realized this only after becoming a mother. Apart from this, I would not change anything. I am extremely proud about having changed the conversation around menstruation and enabling people to think about it in a positive way.

All the major brands were doing *laaga chunari mein daag* kind of communications around periods. We taught people to not associate shame with menstruation and to show it in a positive light. And that, I think, has been our greatest win.

What does your typical day look like?

I begin my day at 5:30 in the morning. After I freshen up, the process of sending my son to school begins. Since I have a house help and a cook to assist me with this, I use the time to get ready for the gym. Tuhin drops our son to the bus stop by 6:30 a.m., and we leave for the gym by 7 a.m. I have a nanny who lives with us and looks after my second child, who is three years old.

Tuhin and I leave for the office by 10 a.m. Our children started attending the office since they were very young, hence we have a dedicated space for them, which we call the Wonder Wing. It has a separate pantry and a play area designed to keep them occupied.

I take a lunch break when my son returns from school and we spend some time together in the Wonder Wing. I speak with a lot of mothers daily because we are also working on an educational game, and a large portion of the work at the moment entails testing user feedback.

Since we work till 7 p.m. or so, the kids leave for the park with my support staff at around 5 p.m. and then they leave for home from there. Tuhin and I walk back home from work, our office being very close to it. We all finish our dinner by 8 p.m. and go to bed by 9:30 p.m. We read to our kids every single night. In between, I try to get some skincare done.

2

"Right now, I am in a phase where I feel a strong need to give back to society more meaningfully"

Ameera Shah

Promoter and Executive Chairperson,
Metropolis Healthcare Limited

If you had asked a young Ameera Shah what she would like to be when she grew up, being the promoter and executive chairperson of India's second-largest diagnostic chain she had founded would definitely not have been her answer. Although her parents were both in the medical field, she had no aspirations for a career in medicine or healthcare as a child. Her father, Dr Sushil Shah, a pathologist, had a standalone pathological laboratory in south Mumbai and her mother, Dr Duru Shah, a gynaecologist, is among the most well-regarded ob-gyns in the city.

Ameera would spend her summer vacations at her father's path lab from eight in the morning to eight in the night, attending to customers, manning the front desk and lending a helping hand. But never would she have thought she would be the one responsible for turning that single laboratory into the behemoth chain of diagnostic labs it is today, spanning not only across India but also across the world.

She had absolutely no interest in becoming a doctor. This decision came as quite a surprise as her parents were well-respected doctors. Her elder sister, Aparna, pursued a career in genetics, but Ameera was clear that science and medicine were not for her. Her parents did not discourage her. She graduated from HR College of Commerce and Economics in Mumbai and then pursued a degree in finance at the University of Texas, Austin. After that, she worked at Goldman Sachs for some time before deciding it was not for her.

This was followed by a short stint at Talenthill, a technology and people start-up in Texas. This gave her the guidance she needed, and she realized this was what she wanted to do—to build something from the ground up. She turned her attention to scale her father's single lab into a nationwide chain. The lab was the most trusted one in the area and had a loyal clientele. She wondered, *How can I make this into an institution that could be spread far and wide?* After all, medical diagnostics was a niche space which did not have diagnostic chains, and which still had individual doctors running their own single diagnostic centres.

Even though she had been helping in the laboratory since her childhood, she had to learn the back-end operations of a diagnostic lab from scratch as there were things that only a technical, trained person could understand. She was barely in her early twenties then. She was clear that if she was going to be in the healthcare industry, she would have to make the effort to familiarize herself with all the terminologies and concepts in order to work effectively and win the respect and trust of everyone she dealt with. First, she needed to streamline the back end, bring in computerization and modernization, and create systems and processes.

This had Ameera facing stiff resistance from long-term employees, suppliers and other stakeholders who thought this young girl did not know what she was doing. They were not used to doing business with younger people, especially a woman. She would handle the front desk to ensure she had face-to-face customer contact so she could exactly understand what issues the customers wanted redressed and incorporate them into her remodelling of the lab and its systems.

Dr Shah's lab had already started offering laboratory services to other labs in Mumbai and nearby towns for specialized tests. From this, the idea emerged to rebrand the institution as Metropolis to reflect a larger institution and its potential to extend across the country.

As a young woman entrepreneur with no medical background, Ameera had to constantly deal with bias from those she approached for business. Potential investors would ask her about her plans for marriage when she was pitching for capital, assuming that she would become disinterested in managing the company after getting married and starting a family.

Finally in 2006, they received their first external funding. From 2006 to 2015, she was instrumental in successfully leading three rounds of investment from PE investors, raising her first round of private equity when she was barely twenty-five. She brought on board marquee private equity investors like ICICI India Venture Fund, Warburg Pincus and Carlyle who believed in the Metropolis growth story and that it would make a return of three to four times on their investments.

She has never shied away from taking risks, and perhaps the greatest one she took was in 2015 when she took on a mammoth personal debt to acquire the majority stake in Metropolis, marking a significant turning point in her life. Ameera, through an LLP called Metz in which she holds 99 per cent stake, repurchased a 27 per cent stake that was held by the private equity firm Warburg Pincus, which they had initially invested way back in 2010. In 2015, Warburg Pincus wanted to sell its stake.

Ameera undertook yet another risk by buying out the Warburg Pincus stake. She borrowed money at a huge rate of interest and pledged 100 per cent of her company shares to buy back the shares. Despite receiving advice from well-wishers against incurring such a substantial personal debt of around Rs 550 crore, she remained adamant. Her unwavering determination was fuelled by her meticulous planning for every conceivable scenario, and her trust in her instincts over others' opinions. She was resolute in her commitment to preserving what she had painstakingly built over the years.

If the risk hadn't paid off, she could have lost the company. However, she successfully navigated through it. As of April 2019, they owned 67 per cent of the shares, but she later sold some to reduce the debt. In the same month, Ameera led the listing of the company on the stock exchange. At the time of writing this, Metropolis Labs has a market capitalization of approximately Rs 11, 500 crore, with an 11 per cent compound annual growth rate (CAGR) for the past seven years. The company was awarded the NABL accreditation (National Accreditation Board for testing and Calibration Laboratories run by the Department of Science and Technology) in 2004 and CAP (The College of American Pathologists) accreditation in 2005, as well as the CLIA certification. Metropolis is rated amongst the top 1 per cent labs across the world for quality in laboratory operations and processes.

The company's extensive footprint spans 28 states, seven union territories and over 800 towns in India, supported by a robust network of more than 220 laboratories, 4,500 service centres, 31 ISO:15189 accredited labs (27 in India, 4 in Kenya), 1 CAP Accredited Lab (India) and over 10,000 touchpoints. Internationally, it is one of the leading diagnostic companies in Africa, with a presence in Kenya, Zambia, Ghana, Tanzania and Uganda. Besides, the company serves hospitals and pathology labs in 12 other countries, including the United Arab Emirates, Mauritius, Nepal, Sri Lanka and Bangladesh. In recent times, Metropolis Healthcare has gone down the mergers and acquisitions route, with three strategic acquisitions.

In March 2025, they acquired Delhi NCR-headquartered Core Diagnostics, a strategic acquisition that will enhance Metropolis's capabilities in advanced cancer testing, while deepening its presence in northern and eastern India and driving market share expansion in the specialized segment across the country. In May 2025, Metropolis acquired Dehradun's leading diagnostic chain Dr Ahujas' Pathology and Imaging Centre (DAPIC), also a leading name in Uttarakhand's diagnostic sector, with a strong B2C presence, making it a valuable addition to its growing network in north India.

In June 2025, Metropolis Healthcare acquired Agra-based Scientific Pathology, founded by Dr Ashok Kumar Sharma, through a business transfer agreement (BTA). This strategic move looked at strengthening Metropolis' presence in western Uttar Pradesh, accelerating its B2C expansion, and unlocking growth opportunities across the state and beyond.

Apart from her responsibilities at Metropolis, Ameera is the president of NATHealth (Healthcare Federation of India), an apex body shaping the future of Indian healthcare. She is an independent director on the board of reputed Indian companies such as Torrent Pharmaceuticals

Limited and ACC Limited (a part of the Adani Group). Prior to the pandemic, she was an advisor to Baylor College of Medicine, Texas, and on the global advisory board of AXA, one of the world's leading insurance and asset management groups, headquartered in Paris with 700 billion dollars under asset management.

She has also served as secretary of the Indian Association of Pathology Laboratories (IAPL) and as the co-chairperson of Federation of Indian Chambers of Commerce and Industry (FICCI) Health Services Committee in 2012. She also went back to college to do the prestigious Owner-President Management Program at Harvard Business School.

She has earned many accolades for what she has built. In 2015, the World Economic Forum named her a Young Global Leader. Ameera was named one of Asia's Power Businesswomen by Forbes Asia in 2020, featured in the Forbes India Tycoons of Tomorrow list in 2018, and recognized among the Fifty Most Powerful Women in Business by both *Fortune India* and *Business Today* consecutively for the past eight years. She is the recipient of the Entrepreneur of the Year Award in healthcare category for the year 2021 from Ernst & Young, making her one of only three women to ever receive this award in the past 20 years and the youngest woman ever to receive this award.

She has also had a brief stint in showbiz, on the start-up reality television show called *The Vault*, as an investor. In 2017, Ameera decided to create a not-for-profit initiative to support women-led businesses through mentorship and micro funding called Empoweress, to create the ecosystem she did not have while starting out. In 2024, she realized that with Empoweress, the work she aimed to do would have been limited in terms of reach and hence joined forces with Delhi-based

The Udaiti Foundation to scale up her dreams of mentoring women entrepreneurs. Managing three young children, a company that is a remarkable success story growing from a single pathology lab and her not-for-profit work in the space of female empowerment, Ameera's is truly an inspiring story of grit, determination and resilience, and of giving back to society.

Excerpts from our interview in 2023 and updated later:

Being the only non-physician in a family of doctors, could you share some childhood memories about growing up with two distinguished doctors as parents and how it influenced you in the path you took? My parents were both incredible medical professionals who built their careers in an extremely ethical manner, tremendously focused on patient care, and would go out of their way for their patients. I have such wonderful memories of growing up as their child, of learning from how they were. My mother, Dr Duru Shah, an obstetrician and gynaecologist, was not only the president of The Federation of Obstetric and Gynaecological Societies of India (FOGSI), but also the president of the prestigious Zonta Club amongst various other things.

I remember at that time the Zonta Club had organized a charity show of the movie *Karma*, and I had lined up all my young friends to go there with donation boxes and encourage the attendees to put some money into those boxes. Like this, I have thousands of memories of being part of so many such events, going for pathology conferences with my father, going for gynaecological events with my mother. So, growing up they were a huge influence.

Dinner-table conversations were about HIV and women's issues and surgeries, and all of that. My parents have always walked their talk.

They have lived their lives with the full value systems they believed in, and left us free to imbibe them as little or as much as we wanted, but have never gave us gyan about how we should be and what we should do. There was full freedom and independence of thought to do exactly what we wanted to do with our lives. There was zero pressure. In fact, I often say, I am the black sheep of the family because I didn't take up medicine. It has been really incredible to grow up in a family of doctors who are such caregivers because that has deeply influenced my outlook on the world.

You studied abroad and joined Goldman Sachs, which was a much-coveted employer for a fresh graduate to be employed at, but you chose to give it up and return to India. What made you take that decision?

It goes back to the independent thought inculcated into me from childhood. Goldman Sachs was like a dream position, and of course, it would be for anyone who was in that field. But when I experienced it, I realized that it was not for me. I had experienced the ability to say that something might look amazing from a distance, but when I experienced it, I could say it doesn't work for me. My parents instilled in me the independence of thought to say, 'Look, you don't have to follow the crowd and you don't have to be a sheep being herded, you can actually choose to be on a different path.'

From the outside, working at Goldman Sachs might look great, but from the inside I hated it. The idea of making money for money just bored the hell out of me. I used to wonder, *Why are people so obsessed with making money?* I simply couldn't get it. The very next year I worked with a start-up in Austin, Texas. There were only five of us. What I loved about it was that in Goldman Sachs I was one of 20,000 and in this start-up I was 20 per cent of the workforce, which meant that if I didn't go to work I was missed. Everything I was doing was relevant and had a direct impact on the business.

It allowed me to do things that were far more strategic rather than being just a paper pusher, as it happens with larger firms. That just gave me a high, the feeling of being relevant, the feeling that I was adding value, and I really enjoyed my work and that is when I realized that my personality is to be a big fish in a small pond versus the other way and I like being a leader. I was a leader from a very young age. Even in school, I was always a prefect.

That was one part of it. The second part was I remember being hugely influenced by Muhammed Yunus of the Grameen Bank. Back in 1997–98, when I was in Austin, I was reading all these articles about Grameen Bank, about social capital, about empowering women, and its impact on world and society and I was just blown away. I thought, *This is amazing*. This is so up my alley, and so resonates with who I am, and I was really captivated. I thought I want to go back to my home country and do something that really makes a difference and adds value to lives.

I believe the reasons I returned to India were the urge to be a big fish in a small pond, the desire to be a leader, the eagerness to have an impact, and the determination to offer value and make a difference.

You took a single lab, your father's lab, and turned it into one of the country's most widespread and trusted diagnostic lab chain. What made you decide to focus on expanding the lab business? What were the challenges you faced, while being from a non-medical background yourself?

When I returned, it was operating as a pathology practice, not a business. My father had his pathology practice, and my mom had her gynaecology practice and both were doing really well for themselves. I asked myself if either of them could be interesting for me, not from a perspective of joining a practice because I didn't have the medical skills to do that, but to take this platform that has been built even if it is just in one part of one city and make it an institution that stood for much more than an individual doctor.

Fortunately, my father had the same vision and since we were aligned and had complementary skill sets, we worked well together in the first few years to move it forward in the direction we wanted. In that regard, pathology definitely had the opportunity to do that, gynaecology did not.

Therefore, I came back with the clear idea of taking Dr Sushil Shah's Lab and Pathology practice and making it something bigger. Did I know where it was going to go? Did I have a blueprint of how I was going to do this? The answer is no. But I did not come back to chew over 'what I was going to do', I came back very specifically to take this on.

I knew that however much I trained I could never become a doctor because informal training cannot take the place of medical training. I was not looking at becoming an expert on the subject but I had to know enough in order to speak where people could relate to me. I had to know what separated a good-quality report from a bad one. What happened behind the scenes, what it was that a doctor was afraid of, what was it that a patient was scared about, from a medical perspective.

I had to spend some time in the lab to understand because there was no structured training programme—it was like I was thrown into the deep sea and I had to swim. It started off with me being at the reception where my job was to manage the customer experience. I was there every day because it was one lab; it was not like there was this big team, and I would face patients, when they came in the morning to give their blood samples and when they came in the evening to pick up their reports.

It was about understanding what they wanted, then actually giving it to them. In the same way, I built the purchase department, I built the IT department. I even started spending time in the lab with all the medical people, and just asked them lots of questions. I learnt as much as I could on the medical side. On the non-medical side too, everything I was doing was new. There was no HR, there was no IT, there was no purchase department, so everything I did was based on common sense.

There were a lot of hurdles. There were a few employees who had been with the lab for over 20 years who thought I was a young kid who was coming here as an intern and hence didn't take me seriously. All the pathologist promoters of all these labs were male, their daughters were my age. A lack of acceptance was the biggest obstacle. I knew I had to earn their respect and trust and this I did by trying to bring to the table what they did not have, while respecting their expertise and knowledge.

What I did have to learn was to adjust to Indian work culture because the work culture in the US was starkly different from India. In the US, people are more blunt, far more direct; if you don't agree with someone you say it straight, and people don't take offence when you disagree with them. Indian work culture is totally different, or it definitely was 20 years ago when I was starting out.

I was 21 and there I was sitting with 65-year-old men and disagreeing with them, asking them to do things differently. While in the US that was completely fine, as everyone had an equal democratic voice, in the Indian culture that was not quite acceptable. In our home, our parents always encouraged us to have a different opinion and there was never really any ego over disagreement, or questions about how could a younger person disagree with us. So I assumed that the rest of the world would be the same, but that was not the case.

That was something I had to learn and figure out over time—how to be tactful and handle things carefully. My nature was to be very straightforward and direct, and so I had to learn how to say things more diplomatically. That took a lot of effort from me, as that was not how I was naturally.

You took a great risk of raising money to get majority in your company. Can you take us through that phase? What made you take that risk and how did you convince yourself to do so?

I had panic attacks. Every morning, I would wake up at three sweating because there was much more going on behind the scenes than just fundraising. I was in a hostile situation, as I faced the risk of my private equity company wanting to exit because it was time for them to do so. I was happy to provide them the exit but someone in the company was trying to block it. Therefore, if I didn't give them one, the plan was to try and sell the company because between the private equity and this person they had majority.

I had to decide whether to allow this to happen or whether there was anything I could do to take control of my destiny. I made the decision to raise the money and purchase the bulk of the company's stock, all the while paying a hefty interest rate. I believed I could really take this to what I believe was my vision and destiny for Metropolis. So, it was a huge punt on myself, it was a huge punt on the business, it was the most scared I have ever been in my life.

It meant I could land up with a Rs 600-crore debt at a 20 per cent interest and have a legal battle on my hands which meant it would be extremely difficult for me to build the business. Hence, I had to really play out every possible scenario in detail and then work the logistics and the execution behind the scenes in such a way so I could do what I needed to do for the business and my family while taking incredible amount of risk.

Tell us a bit about your social work with Empoweress and the Udaiti Foundation.

My mother greatly influenced me with philanthropy work for women in the villages of India. She has written 20 books on women's issues, and has been an incredible force in public policy, in books and in public practice. My mother is an extremely independent, dynamic woman who has done a lot to empower women, which greatly influenced my thinking, growing up.

That was the source of inspiration for Empoweress and I think the Grameen Bank was actually a case study of how you can take that feeling of passion for women and naturally convert it into a socially capitalistic business, which was actually an aha moment for me. How you can bring together passion, purpose and philanthropy into a not-for-profit organization.

Empoweress is about mentoring women entrepreneurs. And I am very passionate about this cause. I know how lonely my journey has been in the last 20 years. This whole bunch of women entrepreneurs has come in the last five-seven years. In the first 15 years of my entrepreneurial journey, there were not that many women entrepreneurs around and frankly growing up in a medical family I didn't have any *chachas, kakas,* uncles, aunts in business and the only people my parents knew were doctors.

So, it was an exceedingly lonely journey for me because I was doing everything myself and from whatever training I had got at business school, which was not so much. Around the years 2012–2013, I realized that I needed mentors and I started reaching out to people to help me build up, and I brought that learning to Empoweress.

I learnt that it was quite a solitary journey, and women especially have a bunch of obstacles. All entrepreneurs face issues with raising funds, having a clear plan, uncertainty, taking risks and not knowing where things are going to go, but women have an additional challenge to overcome the ecosystem that does not support and promote entrepreneurship for them as it does for men.

The kind of support and encouragement that men get from the entire ecosystem, their parents, their family, the fundraisers, women don't get that. Everyone is trying to dissuade the woman from doing it rather than encourage her. The third challenge is our self-doubt where we constantly question our ability to succeed and struggle with confidence.

I felt there was a need for a platform to address all three, where I could provide the mentorship and where we could provide the peer-to-peer learning and group support. While I started doing all this through Empoweress a few years ago, it became immensely difficult during the pandemic as I had a baby to nurture too. Since February 2025, I have been associated with the Udaiti Foundation as an advisor and I look forward to working on female entrepreneurship and empowerment on a much larger scale with them.

You are taking your commitment to women empowerment further by collaborating with the Udaiti Foundation. Tell us about your work with them.

Delhi is going to be a frequent stop for me this year with my engagements at NATHealth and the Udaiti Foundation. When I conceived my twins in September 2023, I had planned that I would take maternity leave through April, May and June 2024, and return to work by July. These were ambitious plans. But as June came to a close, I realized that I had not quite figured everything out. I started feeling highly critical of myself and telling myself I could not just stay at home and had to get clarity on my next steps.

In fact, I had already begun driving mergers and acquisitions conversations from April itself, just a day after returning home from the hospital. So, I told myself, 'Let me focus on just two or three things.' I began looking inward and decided that, for the next three months, I would dedicate myself to helping others in any way I could. That period, from July to September, became a transformational time. Through the process of helping others, I gained a better understanding of what I wanted to do next.

I had always known I wanted to work in the non-profit space and dedicate more time to philanthropy. I also felt strongly about supporting healthcare entrepreneurs, especially those who come from outside the system. Many of them have great ideas and genuine intent, but often fail due to a lack of access to mentorship and guidance. I have been mentoring entrepreneurs informally for eight to nine years now, without ever charging anything for it. I realized I wanted to do more of this in a structured and scalable way.

That is when I decided to take on an advisory role with the Udaiti Foundation, which is focused on increasing women's participation in the workforce for financial empowerment. My specific focus is on creating an ecosystem to support and mentor women entrepreneurs. I am also setting up a centre of excellence for women entrepreneurs under the foundation, which will allow me to channel more of my time and attention towards understanding and addressing the unique barriers women face in building businesses. We aim to closely work with the government to build advocacy and influence policy that truly supports women-led ventures.

Earlier, through Empoweress, I was mentoring female entrepreneurs and facilitating peer-to-peer learning. But I came to realize that one-on-one interactions, while impactful, only go so far. I wanted to amplify that impact. My effort now is to take the same energy and intent and apply it at a systemic level, through policy advocacy, ecosystem building and strategic interventions.

At the same time, I have begun making investments in healthcare and consumer-focused start-ups. I hesitate to call it venture capital in the traditional sense because I believe capital should come with strategic support. I bring what I call 'strategic capital', which is financial backing combined with deep involvement as a friend, philosopher and guide. I support entrepreneurs in making strategic decisions, drawing from my own understanding of the healthcare and consumer landscapes.

I believe life unfolds in phases and stages. Right now, I am in a phase where I feel a strong need to give back to society more meaningfully. These new paths—philanthropy, mentorship and strategic investment—are the ways in which I intend to do that.

What are your plans for Metropolis?

Metropolis today is an institution much larger than me, and I am extremely proud of that. As the business continues to evolve, so will my role within the organization. With my father, Dr Sushil Shah, transitioning into a non-executive role, I took the conscious decision of stepping down as managing director and take on the elevated position of executive chairperson and whole-time director of Metropolis Healthcare.

On the personal front, I decided to undergo IVF in July–August 2023, conceived in September, and delivered my babies in April 2024. Around that time, I had already made the decision to transition into the role of executive chairperson. This shift was not driven by my personal life impacting my professional life, rather it was the other way around. I knew this was the right time to realign my role to focus on the larger strategic direction of the company.

So, my focus is now on strategy, talent, governance, mergers and acquisitions, and crisis management. What that means is that I have more space in my life because I am not running the day-to-day operations of the firm. I am leading it. But I am doing it from a more strategic basis.

In the process of professionalizing the team, we also replaced several senior members and added more talented individuals. The organization has got great professionals and a great team. I have a purpose for it, a vision for it, and that is what building an institution means—you have people who are in sync with your vision for it. They apply their thoughts and ideas keeping in mind the bigger picture. My responsibility right now is to ensure that the soul of the business remains intact, it remains true to its value systems, and we don't lose our way along. That is what I see as my job.

I think the company will do exceptionally well over the next 10 years. The industry currently is perceived to be going through a disruption because of a lot of new competition and increase in competitive intensity; however, that is happening in the categories of the business in which we don't operate so our numbers on the ground in terms of growth and profit are still solid. Metropolis as my first child will continue to do well, I will always be proud of it. But we have really gone into expansion mode. We are now in 750 towns and cities all across the country, and in the next 5 to 10 years we will be at more than 1,000 cities all across India.

We will certainly expand our market influence beyond India into many more markets as well. We will keep diversifying our product mix so that every possible test needed by an Indian is available to them here locally. We will keep trying to make the prices more affordable. I think it is about having purpose on multiple facets of the business.

In addition to developing organically and becoming the industry's fastest-growing player, we have begun our mergers and acquisitions journey, completing three acquisitions in the last few months. We have made it quite evident that we are being extremely fiscally disciplined and cautious when choosing strategic candidates, which will benefit us in the long run. In other words, the terms and the entry price have to be right.

Also, technically and scientifically we were always leaders in the space, but we had ceded space in genomics. We wanted to reclaim it, so we have begun a major campaign to regain our position as leaders in genetics. But I think the biggest learning has been that we are on really, really solid ground. Many companies have tried to enter the market, including hospitals, pharmaceuticals, digital health tech companies. But honestly, all of them are realizing it is much harder to build pathology than they initially believed.

One of the biggest changes has occurred over the past three to four years, beginning in 2021. Back then, if you ask me, we had zero technology-based services. Now, most of our processes are digitized. We are certainly omnipresent to the customer. We are using data to create value. We have made a significant technological shift. Since digital businesses don't lack anything that the excellent incumbents do, they are attempting to enter the bricks and mortar space. The big learning for us has been just that we are on really strong footing and I think we just have to keep doing what we do well.

What is your typical day like?

I get up with the kids around 6:30 to 7:00 in the morning, and I am with them until about 9 a.m. I start working around 10 a.m. I go to the office twice or thrice a week and the rest of the time I work from home. I do this consciously because the stuff not linked to Metropolis can be executed from a separate space. And I want to give space to the teams, I don't want to be sitting there on top of their heads.

On the days I am working from home, if I get five minutes between meetings I go quickly to play with the babies. When my son comes home for lunch we eat together from 1 to 2. Then I work again from 2 p.m. till about 4:30 p.m., when the babies are asleep, and my son, Karma, is busy with his classes. Once I am free, I spend time with all of them till late in the evening. I get a good seven to eight hours with the kids every day, which is great. I also get my six to seven hours of work daily, which is fantastic, and the only thing that gets compromised in all of this is a little bit of me time which I get after 8:30 p.m.

I play chess once or twice a week in the afternoons. I practise by playing with young kids at the chess centre. I make an effort to work out about three to four days a week. I aim to fit that in at 5:30 p.m.; it could be just half an hour of either cycling at home, going for a walk with the kids, swimming or whatever. I usually play badminton or tennis on Saturday mornings, when the kids are busy or asleep.

Luckily, I have a lot of flexibility, so it makes life much easier. I am trying to find just the right balance for myself, and I think it has been really nicely balanced between the emotional energy, the intellectual energy, the spiritual energy and the physical energy.

"Leaders are not defined by their gender so move forward, no matter what"

Anu Acharya
Founder and CEO,
Mapmygenome

She was born in Bikaner, Rajasthan, and grew up on the IIT campus in Kharagpur where her father was a physics professor. Perhaps her career was shaped by her upbringing on campus. Anu was greatly influenced by her father who ensured that she was fascinated by science and technology. He would pay his children small amounts for doing little tasks around the house as he was a firm believer in teaching them the importance of money and hard work. She was always the most enthusiastic among her siblings about completing the tasks.

She would hang out in his lab, listening in to conversations about science and technology between him and his colleagues. They did not have a television and this was the era before mobile phones. Anu would spend her free time reading books, playing basketball and dabbling with science kits. Someday, little Anu told herself, she would win the Nobel Prize. There was always ambition and the urge to be a forerunner in whatever space she chose for herself, right from the beginning. In 1995, she graduated from IIT Kharagpur.

Although Anu had previously been exposed to coding in high school, she learned C and Pascal at IIT. The entire experience thrilled her no end. From IIT, she joined Tata Unisys for barely 19 days when her US visa came through and she left for the US to pursue her master's in physics and MIS (Management Information Systems) from the University of Illinois at Chicago. Here, she learnt both how to code and run a business.

She joined a start-up in Chicago on completing her course. The company created products that let telecom companies port consumers from one telecom operator to another. She worked with Cincinnati Bell on sales and product implementation. She then joined SEI Information, a tech consulting firm, where she worked on a platform to help entrepreneurs connect. She helped a start-up and was working on another project. At around this time, Anu had begun thinking about returning to India.

She was married and already had a baby. She had many ideas about what she wanted to do. She experimented with a few ideas, including VoiceGram, which combines text and voice for mobile devices, and Bandwidth Bazaar, which exchanges bandwidth, with the intention of becoming an entrepreneur. However, these ideas only reached the ideation stage.

In November 2000, Anu moved back to India with a 10-month-old baby, having started Ocimum Bio Solutions with Dr Sujata Pammi, a relative, and Subash Ligareddy, her husband. Sujata had a genomics background. Though registered in the US, it operated out of Hyderabad from 2003.

This was the time the human genome was being sequenced. The Human Genome Project (HGP), a groundbreaking international scientific research initiative aimed at mapping and sequencing the entire human genome, was completed in the same year.

They began building sequence analytical software called Genchek and Genowiz and worked on a lab information software called Biotracker. In 2005, Ocimum began its acquisition spree by accident. The first was a German business to which they intended to sell. The company obtained its first laboratory and purchased two additional genome-related businesses in the US and the Netherlands. Two of the three were publicly listed and one had a valuation of almost two billion a few years ago.

For one of the pitches they were competing against Accenture. Anu and her team promised a third of time and cost when they did not even have the product ready. After many all-nighters they managed to deliver. Optgene, a product for gene optimization, won the innovation prize by the President of India.

Ocimum was essentially a software company that built bioinfomatics and sequence analytics software. It soon became one of the largest service providers in the space in the world. However, most of the data it collected was of Caucasians. Since India did not have the same data, Anu decided to set up Mapmygenome. In 2011, she began work on the algorithms for Mapmygenome and launched it two years later, using money she had saved. The challenge was getting enough data material for Indians. They raised a $1.1 million pre-series A funding, and a founder investment of around $2 million in 2016. Investors like Ratan Tata and Rajan Anandan of Google India were drawn to the concept.

Today, the company is a leading genomics company providing personalized and preventive healthcare solutions. Mapmygenome analyses the genetic makeup of people and gives them a blueprint on how to stay healthy at-home. DNA and microbiome tests empower proactive health management, while diagnostic genomic tests assist healthcare providers.

Anu has steered Mapmygenome towards many honours including the ET Startup Awards, NASSCOM Emerge 50, WSJ's Top Global Startups, Red Herring Asia and Global, and the Pride of Telangana Award.

Apart from this, she serves as a mentor and board member at prestigious institutions like the National Institute of Biomedical Genomics (NIBMG), National Institute of Animal Biotechnology (NIAB), IIT Hyderabad, IvyCap Ventures, CSIR and ABLE. She was recognized as a Young Global Leader by the World Economic Forum in 2011 and as a distinguished alumnus of her alma university, IIT Kharagpur. Not content to rest on her laurels, Anu aims to change 100 million lives with her products at Mapmygenome by 2030. She has set herself a huge challenge, one that she is determined to take head-on and achieve.

Excerpts from an interview conducted online in December 2023:

Tell us about your early years, family and influences. I believe your father had a big impact on you. How did he instil his passion for science in you?

I was born in Bikaner, Rajasthan, and raised in the small campus town in Kharagpur. Growing up, I wasn't just encouraged to ask, 'Why?' I was instructed how to find the answer by dissecting the details like a scientist. And my world revolved mostly around science and technology. I am glad that I grew up in a supportive environment that valued curiosity.

My father, Prof. H.N. Acharya, was not only a researcher and a teacher, but also a scientist who loved to experiment with new things. He sparked my interest in science, experimentation and creating new things. He would frequently urge us to have meaningful discussions in the house, and observed how we arrived with solutions.

An interesting part was that my father used to interview us and our cousins, and record our dreams and aspirations. I remember once saying that I aspired to win the Nobel Prize in physics as I was fascinated by Nobel laureates and physicists like Albert Einstein and Richard Feynman.

I enjoyed doing different things. You could find me playing basketball, conducting experiments in the physics lab or browsing the library at school. It is like playing multiple roles. I always wanted to make a meaningful difference in people's lives. You know you have to aim high.

I always looked up to my brother as well who is incredibly sharp. While my father would painstakingly explain every element, my brother would quickly answer my questions. Strangely enough, I too developed a knack for processing information and finding solutions either quickly or delving deeply into the complexities.

You graduated in physics from IIT and then pursued your master's in the US. What made you switch to information technology?
I graduated with a degree in physics from IIT Kharagpur in 1995 because I aspired to follow in my father's footsteps. I was always encouraged to dig deeper and learn everything with a wider perspective since I was a child. The idea was to be a trailblazer in whatever I did. So, when I realized that I would only be a mediocre physicist, I started

looking for more options. It was a process of self-discovery for me, in terms of identifying my strengths and weaknesses and capitalizing on my talents.

After earning my master's in physics, I enrolled in a master of science in management information systems at the University of Illinois, Chicago. When I moved to Chicago for my master's, I realized that there were many opportunities in the field of information technology, especially in the emerging areas of data science.

I think this combination of physics and IT gave me a unique perspective and skill set that helped me in my entrepreneurial journey.

You worked for a while in the US. What were the learnings from those workspaces and how did they help you when you eventually decided to get into entrepreneurship?

I gained a lot of valuable experience and learnings from those workspaces, which helped me become an entrepreneur. Some of the key learnings were:

- How to work in a multicultural and diverse environment, where people from different backgrounds, cultures and perspectives collaborate and communicate effectively.
- How to use cutting-edge tools and technologies to solve complicated challenges and develop creative solutions by utilizing the power of data and analytics.
- How to adapt to the changing needs and expectations of the customers and the market, and how to be agile and flexible in responding to them.
- How to manage projects and teams, and how to balance the trade-offs between quality, cost and time.

- How to deal with uncertainty and risk, and how to learn from failures and mistakes.
- They also inspired and encouraged me to follow my passion and make a difference in the world.

These learnings helped me develop the skills and mindset that are essential for entrepreneurship, such as creativity, problem-solving, leadership, resilience and vision. They also gave me the confidence and motivation to pursue my passion and create a positive impact in the world.

How did you establish yourself in the biotech space despite being a physicist, and how did you as a woman navigate this highly male-dominated space?

It was quite a big leap from studying physics to deciding on a career in genomics. I am always interested in learning new things and genomics research was fascinating and very novel to India. That become the foundation of Ocimum Biosolution, a pure bioinformatics company that evolved to become a fully functional genomics outsourcing partner for several large pharma and biotech companies and eventually became one of the largest globally.

With the encouraging developments of the Human Genome Project (HGP), our efforts began to bear fruit. I gained knowledge of the basics of biology and genetics, and I collaborated with experts and researchers in the biotech domain. Additionally, I made use of cutting-edge platforms and technologies including artificial intelligence, cloud computing and machine learning.

What started as a pure bioinformatics company soon became an enterprise with top pharma labs using our RaaS (Research as a

Service), solutions, genomics database, customised LIMS and TB diagnostics kits. Ocimum became one of the largest service providers in the genomics space for discovery, development and diagnostics with three international acquisitions and two fund raises.

How did you decide to get into entrepreneurship, and what were the learnings from your first two enterprises?

After returning to India at the end of 2000 to launch Ocimum Biosolutions, we brainstormed several venture ideas including Bandwidth Bazaar for bandwidth trading and VoiceGram which was based on the idea of integrating voice and text mobile. Bioinformatics was domain-heavy and brand new and intellectually stimulating, and that was exactly what I was looking for.

I think entrepreneurship is not just about great ideas, it is about perseverance and dedication. It is about pushing your abilities and discovering your passion. Choose the problem for which you wish to find a solution.

How did the idea of your venture, Ocimum, come about, and how did you manage to grow it?

I was fascinated by the emerging field of genomics and bioinformatics as it provided us with the very software of our own lives. The four letters, A, T, C and G, representing the four chemical bases adenine, thymine, cytosine and guanine that make up the DNA, which helps create life as we know it, would need a lot of programming to unravel its mysteries.

I saw an opportunity in this space that could provide solutions for genomics research and drug discovery. We would say curiosity was in our genes and we were eager to see how much the world could benefit from the growing landscape of genomics. We grew with acquisitions and a vision to enable R&D across the world and had most of the large pharmaceutical and biotech clients as our own.

You established Mapmygenome after Ocimum, which was a totally different service and a pioneer in the field. What made you decide to launch a business and what were the problems that you faced?
By 2012, the company had built a huge database on pharmaceutical drug usage and gene expression. However, most of the work we were doing wasn't impacting the average person in India. Genomics was just about starting in the clinic and I was motivated to reduce the genomic inequality that existed in the world. I also realized that I wanted to do something more meaningful and personal in the field of genomics.

During that time, a lot of research was being conducted in the field of personalized medicine. The idea of developing genomic databases—a cross-referenced compilation of genetic data—and its potential to aid in disease prevention came to me as a result.

Furthermore, I discovered that while India accounts for 1/6th of the world population, the data for Indians was less than 0.2 per cent. This led me to start Mapmygenome in the year 2013 in Hyderabad, with my own savings. We unveiled Genomepatri, our flagship product, a DNA test for wellness and health.

There was a significant disconnect when we first started. People thought genetic testing was about finding your biological parents or identifying rare disorders. We had to present them with an alternative— the application of genetic knowledge to everyday health and well-being.

Finding local expertise was one of the primary obstacles we faced when we started Mapmygenome because genomics was still in its infancy in India. I looked at the regulations in other countries and tried to abide by them, as the framework in India was unclear.

Obtaining sufficient data, appropriate genetic markers and research material about the Indian population was another. We had to deal with the insufficiency of Indian genomics data. Our bioinformatics team did a great job in creating the right algorithm and reports, and we continue to evolve. We are now able to raise awareness of the need of genetic testing and build the largest collection and curation of Indian data.

How have you been upgrading your product offerings and how difficult is it to get retail customers to buy this and do the tests? Mapmygenome has evolved into a full-stack genomics company with two verticals—preventive and clinical genetic tests. We offer a range of products and services that help people discover their genetic potential, understand their health risks and take proactive steps to improve their health outcomes.

We also aim to create a culture of preventive healthcare in India, where people are more conscious of their health status and act before it is too late. Genomics can empower people to make informed choices about their health and lifestyle, and we believe that prevention is the cure.

When did you decide to raise funds and what has your fundraising journey been like? Tell us about your first fundraising experience in 2015. Did you come up against implicit biases because you were a woman in this space? If so, what were your learnings from the experience?

We did not have much difficulty in raising the initial round of funding, but it was challenging to raise a large amount of money later on. We had some people who reached out to us, but our aim was to find the right investors who could help us grow the business. We were looking for the right partners and the ideal board that could relate to our work and help us find the right prospects.

Yes, I did come up against biases because of my gender, but I chose to ignore them and focus on my path.

Some of our well-known investors include Rajan Anandan, Arihant Patni and Ratan Tata. Having the late Ratan Tata as one of our investors was amazing. He was extremely interested in our work and had read everything we had written on the product pitch deck.

It was wonderful to speak with him and to know that he appreciated and recognized the significance of our work and its influence on the nation and society. Having people like him on board made all the difference.

We only selected investors who shared our vision and long-term objectives. They supported us and trusted us throughout our journey.

Do you have any plans to launch any new products?

We have already launched three innovative products: MedicaMap, BeautyMap and MapmyBiome.

Our ongoing work in epigenetics looks into how our living environment and lifestyle affect our genes. While ageing is a natural phenomenon, various environmental and lifestyle factors accelerate it. By studying epigenetic modifications, we learn more about how to prevent or treat diseases that are linked to genes and gain insights into ways to potentially reverse or slow down our biological ageing processes through personalized interventions.

How crucial is it for women to have support from family and loved ones when they start their own business? What advice would you give women who are becoming entrepreneurs about building up their support system?

No doubt support from family and loved ones is crucial for anyone getting into entrepreneurship. Entrepreneurship is a challenging and demanding journey that requires a lot of hard work, dedication and perseverance. It also involves a lot of uncertainty, risk and stress. Having a supportive and understanding family and loved ones can make a huge difference in coping with these challenges and maintaining a healthy balance between work and personal life.

My advice for women who are planning to be entrepreneurs is to build a support network by communicating their goals and aspirations to their family and loved ones, and seeking their feedback and encouragement. They ought to look for mentors, role models and peers who can guide, inspire and motivate them.

They should network with other women entrepreneurs and join communities and platforms that can provide them with resources, opportunities and connections. They should also not hesitate to ask for help when they need it and to celebrate their achievements and milestones with their supporters.

And one more thing, leaders are not defined by their gender so move forward, no matter what.

What is your typical day like and how do you relax?

My typical day is quite busy. I usually start my day with yoga or a morning walk. Then I catch up on my emails and head to the office. My schedule has a bunch of internal and external meetings and these days also a lot of Zoom talks/podcasts.

I unwind by spending quality time with my family and friends. I enjoy solving puzzles, sometimes watching movies or series and listening to music. I also like to travel and love writing poetry. I also enjoy savouring different teas and experimenting with their flavours and blends. I think I got a pair of brew genes.

My love for tea began at home as my parents were chai lovers. My mom has her very own recipe for masala chai which consists of cardamom, ginger, pepper, javitri, nutmeg and cinnamon. She uses tulsi and brahmi during winter, which probably made me a tea drinker. Dad appealed to the nerd in me by telling us about its properties and how this would be good for memory.

And finally, what kind of legacy do you hope to leave behind?

Let us keep it simple. Mapmygenome and I want to help healthy people stay healthy and support them to become healthier using genomics and innovative technologies. Our goal is to touch 100 million lives and save a million by 2030.

Our goal is to create a space that combines innovation, excellence and social good. The fact that people come and tell us how the genetic tests and preventive measures have helped them in their lives keeps us going. I want people to be empowered and help them know that they have greater control over their health. So, your health is worth being curious about. It is a smart move for your future and your genes can give you a head start.

4

"It is important for women to understand that they can juggle work and home successfully"

Apurva Purohit
Co-Founder,
Aazol

It takes guts to walk away from the boardroom and to start over, especially when one is in one's fifties. It takes even more courage to walk out of the corporate world where one has made one's mark to set up an enterprise in a field that is completely different from what one has done all one's life. And then, to weave it in with a social cause, put in one's own money to see it through.

Would one call it courage or foolishness? After all, most people would kill to be as successful as she was when she decided to give it all up and start a food product business that closely worked with self-help groups (SHGs) from rural Maharashtra. Apurva Purohit would laugh aloud and say it was a mix of both. She is, and has always been, a woman who never minces her words, whether in the boardroom or out of it.

She was all of 55, when at the height of the pandemic that had brought the world to its knees, she took the rather sudden decision to quit from her position as president of Jagran Group and set up

Aazol. It might have appeared to be a leap of faith, but it was one that had been years in the making. The pandemic after all had a lot of people rethinking their life goals and passions, and for her too, this was a moment of reckoning. She had reached the pinnacle of a career studded with glory. Where to from here?

The only answer it would seem was to strike out on her own. And, more importantly, to give back to society. With that single move, Apurva checkmated all those who had been watching her career with interest.

She had a stellar journey that had inspired many young women embarking on their careers in the corporate world. The accolades had been plentiful but she wore them lightly. She was ready to move on into a space she had never been in before, and along with her for the ride was her son, Siddharth.

Born on 3 October 1966, Apurva grew up all over the country thanks to her father's job with the Oil and Natural Gas Corporation (ONGC). Her mother was a teacher. She lived in Mumbai, Ahmedabad, Assam, Chennai, across the country, imbibing all the cultural and linguistic diversity that went into the making of the syncretic fabric of our nation. She excelled academically and worked hard, graduating in physics from Stella Maris College in Chennai, where she also played hockey for the state. She then pursued MBA at the Indian Institute of Management in Bangalore.

It was here, at IIMB, that she met Sanjay Purohit, whom she later married. After earning her MBA, she decided to pursue a career in advertising instead of looking for a position in one of the multinational FMCG groups or banks. From an internship at Hindustan Thompson in her last year of her MBA programme, to joining Rediffusion, then

Ulka, where she was responsible for setting up Lodestar, a media buying agency, the first of its kind in the country, she found a natural affinity with media and numbers.

She then moved to Zee TV where she oversaw the relaunch of the group's flagship channel, Zee TV, which had seen a beating with the advent of several competing networks. She left Zee to work as chief operating officer of Times Television at Bennett, Coleman and Company Limited where she oversaw Times Group's highly anticipated entry into television in 2004 with Zoom TV, pegged as India's first lifestyle channel. She moved then to Radio City, where during her roughly 10 years as CEO, she spearheaded its expansion in the FM radio market, successfully oversaw its 2017 stock exchange listing and is recognized with the company's successful first public offering.

For many years, Radio City was also recognized as one of the best places to work for women, and was listed in the Great Place to Work survey. When it was acquired by the Jagran Group in 2015, Apurva came onboard as the president of Jagran Prakashan, overseeing the entire business operations and functioning of *Mid-day*, Inext, Jagran online and other non-print businesses besides Radio City. It was a huge mandate, and one that she led with great aplomb.

In 2021, in the thick of a global pandemic, she launched Aazol Ventures Pvt Ltd, along with Siddharth, a consumer products company that sells traditional food items made by SHGs and micro entrepreneurs. The name Aazol itself comes from the Marathi word for one's maternal grandparents' home. Aazol has around 30 products such as chutneys, masalas, peeths and papads sourced from almost 25 SHGs and women micro entrepreneurs across Maharashtra.

With Aazol, Purohit found the perfect synergy between her need to create something to empower women financially, and her son's need to work in a space to promote environmental sustainability. Despite no prior experience in the food industry, she managed to turn the disadvantage to her advantage, because as she puts it, 'If you don't know that people think that something can't be done, you have nothing to hold you back. You just go ahead and do it.' Her desire to give back to society and create a venture that benefits all parties involved has already led to more jobs in rural areas and a reversal of numerous women's migration to urban areas. Purohit is also the author of the two bestselling books on women empowerment in the workplace, *Lady, You're Not a Man: The Adventures of a Woman at Work* and *Lady, You're the Boss!* She is also an independent director at LTIMindtree, L&T Technology Services, Navin Fluorine International Ltd and Marico.

She has received numerous accolades throughout her corporate career. She has been named as one of the Most Powerful Women in Business by the India Today Group and Fortune India. She was listed among LinkedIn's Top Voices and YourStory's Top 10 digital Influencers of 2020. In 2022, she was awarded the Distinguished Alumni Award from IIM Bangalore.

In 2016, 2018 and 2019, *Business Today* named her one of the top 30 most powerful women in business. In 2018, 2019 and 2020, she was listed among *Fortune India's* Most Powerful Women in Business. And with her stepping into the entrepreneurial space, one can be assured that Aazol will be a venture to watch in the years to come. And more importantly, a venture that gives back to women in a way that empowers and dignifies them.

Excerpts from an interview conducted in September 2023 in Mumbai:

Please share a bit about your childhood and growing years, the influences that shaped you.

As you grow older, you start reflecting on your childhood a bit more. Otherwise, you think your identifiable life-altering milestones only occur after you become an adult. However, I have recently started thinking about how much our foundations impact us throughout our lives. It is only now that the dots have been connected and this awareness has occurred.

My parents came to India after the partition. During the pandemic, when my extended family gathered, we realized that the older generation was gradually passing away and that our history was vanishing along with them. Without them and their memories our past was essentially a blank canvas because my parents were abruptly uprooted from their hometowns. My father grew up in Bombay, my mother in Chandigarh and our upbringing was all in the metros. Since we did not live in a joint-family setup we had little idea about their lives before their marriage.

You now understand that when they left Pakistan they left behind not only all their wealth but also a great deal of legacy and ancestry. My paternal grandfather was a a founding member of Punjab Bank and Multan Electricity Board, and we had no clue. They came to India, leaving everything behind. My paternal grandmother, a widow with six children, was uneducated, but incredibly intelligent and perceptive.

She got her daughters married off into good families one by one, her sons educated, and one of my aunts became a doctor and was educated in the UK back then. I only learned about all of this in the last two or three years after reading about our family in the stories of a book privately published by our family, so that was the type of background our parents had. They put in a great deal of effort because they had to start over from scratch.

It has been 25 years since my father, a government official, died at the age of 65, but I do remember him as being very motivated and hardworking, without a family member or mentor to help him along the way. He was a self-made man. The absence of grandparents can result in not having any support and mentorship to push you ahead in life's race.

In short, it was only hard work and education that got our parents so far and the value of these was drilled into our minds. So getting proper education became a huge part of our upbringing. It was important for us to top our class, it was important for me to get through IIM and for my brother to get through IIT and become an engineer. We were constantly reminded of that. Since my mother was a teacher, discipline was strictly instilled. I never bunked school, for example. I would get up at six in the morning to have a bath even on weekends! The erratic water supply was partly the reason I had to bathe at such ungodly hours.

My parents were government employees, so we stayed in government colonies, and since they kept getting transferred, we have lived in Mumbai, Chennai, Assam, Gujarat and Ahmedabad. They would get transferred every three years. Our longest stint was in Mumbai where we stayed for five to seven years. The problem with these frequent transfers is that you don't develop enduring relationships or roots. I see a lot of people saying, *'Yeh toh hamarey bachpan ke dost hai, hamarey bachpan ke dost bane hi nahin ya bicchade gaye jaldi* because we kept getting transferred.

But the good part is you get to live in different regions of the country and learn about their cultures. This experience greatly helped me when I was running Radio City, as I was much more aware of the cultures of different cities which allowed me to connect the radio stations' programming to diverse cultures. Thus, the cultural understanding of different parts of the country came far easier to me. The other important thing was that we never grew up thinking *yeh to Gujarati hai, yeh Punjabi hai, yeh Maharashtrian hai.* We were all from the ONGC family. Until I got married, I didn't know these distinctions.

So, I was astonished when I heard, *'Arrey yeh toh Gujarati hai, isliye aisa hai'* or *'Achcha Bengali hai to aisa hoga'.* This happened after I got married at the age of twenty-two. I had never heard such statements before. Therefore, I get agitated about what is happening around us because we are all part of one country, we are all one.

My mother, who has an almost genius-level IQ, was working towards a PhD in psychology when she got married and had to abandon her thesis submission. She was compelled to get married because her younger sister wanted to get married. She studied science, she was the only female student in the science college at that time.

She had to go with some staff to sit in the class because she was the only girl. She had a lot of drive and ambition, but she was unable to really pursue a career because my father was always getting transferred. But she worked as a teacher. She also studied arts because psychology interested her. So, she could teach science, she could teach maths, she could teach arts. She could teach almost any subject.

How did sports impact you in the lessons you learnt for life?
I do not want to give the standard responses, such as teamwork and discipline though they are obviously true. I was not a sporty person at all in school. In college I was forced to pick up a sport, and once I had selected hockey I pushed myself and got into the school team, the college team, the university team, the state team. I am a typical Type A personality.

Therefore, it gave me the confidence that if you persevere you can succeed in whatever you choose to do. If a completely non-sporty person like me can get into the state team, anyone can. I still believe I got into IIM because I was playing sports at that time. Not because it was a tick mark at the interview stage, but I remember we would get up at six in the morning for practice, practise from 6–9, attend college from 9 a.m. to 2 p.m., then from there I would go to the classes for the IIM entrance exams from 4 p.m. to 7 p.m., return home at 7 p.m., then there were studies again, projects, homework, etc.

This was the routine on weekdays. On the weekends, we went to play matches in Salem, North Arcot and some very small places in the state where there weren't even toilets for girls sometimes. I feel today what that did was make the mind and body stretch with hard work and increase my mental agility and speed. The CAT after all is an exam where your mind has to be working at full speed in a limited time. You have to answer 100 questions, and you have negative marking. I believe that if any part of my body had been loose and lazy, my mind would not have been as sharp.

Did you ever envision yourself as a corporate woman? There were no role models back then. How then did you shape your career?

I was good at my studies. My mother pinned all her hopes on me as I was the oldest child. I did not let her down. I was intelligent, hardworking, studious and quite nerdy. If you go to Duruelo Convent, in Bandra, Mumbai, you can still see my name as the topper there, for the year I passed out in my tenth boards, 1981.

One of my cousins at that time had studied from IIM and then joined Citibank. Citibank back then was the ultimate corporate entity, so my mother would say, 'Look at her, that is what I want you to do.' It was drilled in my mind since the sixth or the seventh standard that I had to get into an IIM. She never explicitly stated which career she wanted me to take up, but she wanted me to get through IIM, as IIM and IIT were the defining symbols of intelligence and future success. The fact that it was the gateway to the corporate world was not explicitly stated. So, I gave the CAT, and I was accepted to IIM Bangalore.

It was at the IIM I realized that I want to work and have a career. I can't actually articulate why I felt so. Except, I was very clear that I didn't want to stay at home and just manage a house. This desire was very inherent. I got married after graduating from IIM. I was only 22 then and my husband was a year older. We didn't really think too much about it, we liked each other and both felt equally passionate about each other's careers and growing in the corporate world which was going through its phase of liberalization in the early 1990s. Even after having a baby, our careers remained equally important to both of us.

My mother used to say, 'I want you to have a career and when you have a child. I will give up my job and take care of your child.' Now when I look back and reflect, I feel so sad because she was so passionate about teaching and she cried so much when she left. She was a professor at St Andrew's, Mumbai. She left her job and assured me, 'I will take care of Siddarth, so don't worry.' That kind of support was critical.

I, of course, enjoyed working. I loved it. Of course, there was politics and toxicity at the workplace but I enjoyed most of my jobs and I kept getting better opportunities all throughout my career, which helped me develop as a leader early on.

You introduced new concepts in media planning and buying by setting up Lodestar, which was the first of its kind. How did that come about?

From Rediffusion I moved to FCB Ulka, which was known as Ulka at the time. Rediffusion was a typical agency with long lunches with clients and full of cool people. But I was not a cool person. All of them used to stay in Bandra and South Bombay and I used to stay in Goregaon. I would rush home after work. After all, I was married. They were partying and I was running a household! So in that sense, I wasn't a typical advertising person of the '90s. I enjoyed working with the clients and brand strategy a lot. For example, in a campaign for Palmolive soap with Aamir Khan, we launched the notion of skin care for the first time, explaining to the customers that there are different soaps for different types of skin and that there are oily and dry skin types.

While I was at Ulka, agencies were beginning to divide their media and creative departments. I enjoyed the maths part of media. I enjoyed the creative bit too, but I enjoyed this part more given my science background. My bosses figured out my leadership qualities early on. Nobody used to do my KRA as my bosses would be confused about who is the boss. Shashi Sinha, who was my boss at that time, still says the jury is out as to who was the boss. [*Apurva laughs loudly.*] One fine day they told me to head a new division. That was how Lodestar came about.

We started out by first doing media operations, then media planning and then media buying.

From Ulka and Lodestar, you moved to Zee and BCCL both of which were very proprietor led. What kind of mental shifts did you have to do to adapt to a proprietor-driven work culture?

Since they were proprietor led, they were not very process-oriented. Things happened quite whimsically. *Kaun Banega Crorepati* had just been launched. Zee was going through a very bad phase. There was a great deal of worry at Zee because it had dropped from the number one position. I recall having to make judgments quickly and attempting to adapt to a rapidly changing climate where, after years of being in the leadership position, the channel lost its rankings suddenly. The good part was that you had the flexibility of making quick decisions, some of which turned out to be quite successful.

You learnt to deal with pressure. Whims and fancies were present, but they were tamed by the bigger issue that we had to react rapidly and get changes done quickly. Whereas, when I went to the Times Group after Zee, I realized how the environment revolved a lot around the promoter.

When we launched Zoom as a niche lifestyle channel in 2003, within five days people were congratulating me. But I was perplexed. We didn't have any TRP ratings, so on what grounds were they claiming success? When I asked around I got the reply: 'No, no, the boss likes it very much.' Then I realized that in their mind whatever the boss liked was a success, what the boss didn't like was a failure. I found that quite strange.

Both these organizations had a lot of senior women, but I was the first female director. There were enough women, women DJs, women models, women handling programming. There were women editors. Both places gave me the freedom and the space to run my thing, so I didn't feel any sense of bias there.

You became president of the Jagran Group. You transformed it from a largely print-led organization to one that fully embraced new media and technologies. As a leader, what kind of resistance did you face from the old guard and how did you push forth? What kind of resistance came purely because you were a woman?
Interestingly, the patriarchal and the proprietor-led organizational issues that I spoke about earlier, I faced most at Jagran. It was a family-based company with family members in charge of various divisions. There was resistance of course when I suggested moving into the digital space because there was a traditional way of doing things, and print was the bread and butter of the organization. Print has a different way of doing things, reporters came in late, filed a single story a day whereas for digital we needed a constant stream of stories all through the day. So, there was a lack of understanding earlier and the resistance to change. My biggest challenge was to ensure that the culture of Radio City wasn't lost in the merger, and then leading it to a successful IPO. And there was the challenge of integrating *Mid-day*, which had been a strong brand in the English tabloid space in the metros, with the larger ecosystem.

What made you think of becoming an entrepreneur at the age of 55, especially when you doing so well professionally. Did you ever feel the doubts of setting out on a completely new path at this stage in your life?

I am a firm believer in the age-old tenet that there are various stages of your life: 25 years you are a student, then 25 years you are a householder, etc. I am in that phase where I want to give back to society. I have also been inspired by the emerging breed of philanthropists, who have been professionals like me who have reached the pinnacle of corporate success and are now giving back to society. One such example is Subroto Bagchi. He has built companies and is now such a prominent social leader who works with the government, is a philanthropist and shapes destinies.

You must also remember that my growth story in the corporate world began early. While my peers were only just becoming CEOs, I had been there, done that long ago. So, it was time for me to step back, to give back. At the same time, Siddharth was back from the US, fed up with consulting and keen to begin something in the environment and sustainability space, which was his area of interest. He pushed a lot for me to join him as a co-founder.

Every year, there was this exhibition by SHGs on the grounds at Bandra Kurla Complex where they showcased their food products. The products were poorly packaged, they had no clue about marketing, but the quality of the products was absolutely excellent. We got to thinking that perhaps there was an opportunity here, to help women as I wanted to, and to promote environmentally-friendly, sustainable food brands, in keeping with Siddharth's interests.

He travelled throughout Maharashtra to meet these SHGs and gain insights into how they created their products and what could make them stay with the traditional produce they were growing rather than switching to what was popular. For instance, if the farmer sees there is a demand for basmati rice he stops growing the native rice of the region and switches to basmati which may not be friendly to the soil. Like, say, an Indrayani rice is a brilliant endemic rice, a sticky rice, much better than this jasmine rice which we keep importing.

Eating more locally grown, natural, seasonal food that fits your genes and DNA is better for you from the standpoint of your carbon footprint, local economy and what your bodies need. We therefore determined that this is the area that interests us after considering the environmental and women's perspectives, as the majority of SHGs were driven by women. I think sometimes ignorance is bliss so without much ado we launched with 20 products straightaway. [*Her eyes twinkle.*] That was a blessing in disguise because I think if you know the industry you are more sceptical, more cautious. When you jump in without testing the waters, you will either sink or swim.

Interestingly, despite me coming into this with the aim of giving back from a place of philanthropy, my son said something to me that has been with me ever since: 'Mummy, don't ever come with this white knight syndrome. We are not knights coming to save the SHGs—they are our partners, they are making excellent products, they are leading an ideal lifestyle, staying in villages, eating fresh food and breathing clean air.'

What they don't have is money to improve their lot. You do need money to put a water pump in your village, you do need money to hire a school teacher for the village school. You need access to markets and supply chains and thus access to money was what they were missing. That is why they are where they are. Poverty has different definitions. They have economic poverty, not lifestyle poverty.

They are our partners, they make excellent products, and our job is to market them. That is why I never say that I am running an NGO. It is my philanthropic endeavour, but the business is not an NGO. I tell everyone to buy the products and, of course, to support the women, but more importantly because they are excellent items. They come with great taste and health benefits. Our focus is on these factors.

You opted to not look for funding. Would you be looking at raising funding as you scale up the business?

I don't want to go down this path of start-up, build, scale, unicorn, list, make money, valuation. Valuation is not my game. Ultimately, I want to make this a cooperative, similar to Amul—a cooperative where the employees have ownership, the SHGs have ownership, they have a share. Yes, we want to be profitable and scale but it all needs to get ploughed back. That is what I want to do. The moment Siddharth and I decided this, funding, etc., became irrelevant because everyone will want an exit and there was no plan for an exit.

Secondly, we are fortunate to have the resources, and this is our way of giving back. Others may set up a hospital or a school, I said that I will set up a business where I will use my money. We are blessed to have made the amount of money we have since we started. But what good is it if we don't use it to help others climb the economic ladder?

Although Aazol is our charitable endeavour, it is a professionally run business because only a profitable business can stay the course, become sustainable and impact a wider community.

How difficult was it to launch a business during the pandemic, especially in a field that was entirely unfamiliar to you.

There were disadvantages and advantages. The largest benefit was the enormous increase in the number of consumers who began making purchases online as a result of the digital conversion or acceptance. There was no option, one couldn't go to shops, so it was critical to build up the trust factor—that this was not a scam, if you buy the product online it will reach home. Indians are generally worried and sceptical about whether what they have ordered is what they will receive at home.

That helped many digital brands. The challenge was that you are creating a team which was going to run this business and you were not even seeing them because someone was sitting in Delhi, someone was sitting in Ahmedabad and someone was sitting in Nashik. How do you build a team, create a culture and get them to think the same way? So that was very challenging, and naturally it took extra time.

Also, the supply chain was broken because no one was visiting the warehouse during the pandemic. So those were the challenges. Of course, those got smoothened out after the lockdown was lifted.

Aazol began as a primarily online offering, now you do have some offline presence. Are you looking at expanding your footprint pan-India?

It is becoming apparent to people that omnichannel is the way to go. So you get to be a D2C brand but there are enough people who will never buy online and there are enough people who will never go into a store. India, we know, is a very complex ecosystem. You have to have both a digital as well as an offline presence. So, we are in both the online space as well as in stores, not our own but in stores like Reliance stores, Nature's Basket, Society, etc.

For aspiring women entrepreneurs reading this, what would you like them to know about entrepreneurship and the journey, the pitfalls, the struggles, as well as the joys? How would you prepare them, so to speak?

There are three types of women entrepreneurs. There is the kind who is in this just to ensure some financial independence. For example, there will be someone who will get suits from Jaipur to sell in Mumbai. They are not chasing any big dreams but they do want to be independent.

Then there is someone who is deeply passionate about a particular aspect—travel, art, horticulture, nutrition and wants to be a solo-preneur in that field. If that is what gives you happiness, if that is what gives you joy, it is totally fine. Many times, niche businesses can be very fulfilling. You have to only concentrate on creating an excellent product and an enjoyable customer-delight experience.

Then there is another set of businesses that can scale and should scale. Here the challenge is that many entrepreneurs, especially women, struggle with scaling. Women are a lot more hesitant. Now for scale, you have to be willing to add resources and take risks. When we were starting out, Siddharth advised me to start by hiring a personal secretary and an office boy. I was unsure about doing so given my middle-class upbringing. I asked myself, *Do I really need these people just when we are starting off?* But is filling out visa forms a better use of your time than brainstorming on the business you are starting?

It is not a good use of your time. Secondly, you are creating jobs when you hire staff. You are helping people run families. Invest resources where you should. You can't be a one-woman show, you have to create a team. Look at Aazol, now. We have moved so far ahead from that inability to take the risk of hiring even two employees.

The old Apurva who was a professional all her life, with her saving 50 per cent of her salary, transitioned into someone willing to let her cash burn as she invested in the business. My mind shift has happened. I know our money is being used as an investment in building a legacy business and creating a multitude of jobs in rural Maharashtra. And that is okay.

You must make that mind shift to say, *theek hai* I am growing this business, I have to put in the resources. Sometimes you have to get resources from outside, sometimes you have to get them from within. I think the willingness to do that, and why should you not, today money is easily available, and for women entrepreneurs there are so many opportunities so take them.

You have written two national bestsellers,* Lady, You're Not A Man *and* Lady, You're the Boss. *You wrote these at the peak of your corporate career. What drove you to write them? What do you hope the women who read them will take away?
I wrote these books because I wanted to give a guidebook to women. Our generation and the generation that has come after us lacked women role models who were working and also were managing homes. Either we had mothers who stayed at home or aunts who were working and never got married. This idea that you can do both was new. Even now, there are not enough women doing both. It is important for women to understand that they can juggle work and home successfully.

Why should only a woman be asked about her plans for her career after marriage? Why not the man? Why do women want to work only till they get married? Why do they feel guilty about going to work leaving their child at home? I read a research report that concluded that children of working women are less developed or mature. It was pure nonsense. I was outraged by it and shot off an angry letter to the publication. As it is, women feel guilty.

Now they are making them feel that their children will suffer too. In my opinion, children of working women become more independent, they learn to respect women more and consider women to be equal partners. And that was why I wrote both the books. Even now I get letters from readers.

Recently, a woman wrote on a big social media platform about how she was a theatre artist and unsure about what she wanted to do in life until she discovered *Lady, You're Not a Man*. It changed her life. I was thrilled.

Of all the many awards and accolades you have won, which one is the most precious and why?

I should say two actually. The first one was the first time I was on the Powerful Women list. I was managing sizable companies, but for some reason media businesses were always thought of as not as serious as running a bank or a financial service or an insurance company. Media was seen as a little frivolous. I was running something that was large and complex but was not recognized as such. So, when I got that award the first time it was like a validation of the media business as a serious business.

The second award was the IIM Bangalore Distinguished Alumni award because here I was competing with extremely accomplished peers and mostly males at that. Out of the 120 students in our cohort, nine were girls. That feeling of always being an outsider, a different person, not part of the ecosystem because of my gender was inherent in me. Thus, this award was definitely valuable.

What are your plans for Aazol?

I am very much focused on Aazol. We want to move to a stage where it becomes profitable and then scale it up sustainably. Right now, we are focusing on profitability, not scale. I want young entrepreneurs who are busy running the valuation race to know it is not the only race they need to run. Making their business a sustainable profitable one should also be their goal. Hence, that has been our main focus.

I eventually want to make it an organization that is owned by employees and partners. Siddharth and I are spending a lot of time on achieving this goal.

On the personal front, I have realized that we women rush through juggling work, home, family, which ends up taking a toll on our system. It has been two years since I have left the corporate world. For two years, I continued to function by waking up early, quickly finishing chores and rushing off to work when there was no reason to pack my day so intensely. I had to really force myself to slow down.

Slow down not because you are ageing, but because your nervous system needs to calm down. A hyperactive nervous system impacts our sleep, our digestive system and our mind. It is taking me a lot of time to unlearn this aspect of being on constant alert, with my muscles all tensed up, that is not good. So, right now it is just learning to slow down. We recently bought a farm where we try to spend every weekend amidst nature. Calming down and relaxing is an important part of my personal journey now.

What is a typical day in your life now as an entrepreneur?
My weekdays are quite regimented because I am a creature of habit and regularity. Mornings are spent doing some form of exercise like walking, yoga and strength training. I have a light breakfast around 9 and am off to work by 10 a.m. I make an effort to have breakfast with a buddy, mentee or even a co-worker a few times a week. Fortunately, one of the perks of being an entrepreneur is that you can choose where to have your office; thankfully, my office is a 10-minute drive away.

I work from 10 in the morning until 5 in the evening and then am back home. I do some light relaxation exercises in the evening, chat with my mom and sister and then I have an early dinner by 6:30 or 7 p.m. I watch television for some time, especially movies and shows on crime fiction as I am a big fan of the genre. And when my husband comes home, we spend some time together, and then I catch up on reading before going to bed by 10 p.m. I have sleep issues so I avoid doing anything strenuous or demanding on weeknights, so no socializing, etc.

We typically spend our weekends in Mumbai socializing or in Karjat, where we have a farmhouse.

5

"In terms of planning, execution and fundraising, I would say think big, start small and execute fast"

Ayushi Gudwani
Founder and CEO,
FableStreet (FS Life)

It all started with the campus placement interviews. Ayushi Gudwani, who preferred Western wear, hunted high and low to find great professional Western clothes she could wear for the interviews. At this point she wondered why there was no brand catering to the Indian woman who was in the corporate space looking for smart and comfortable Western wear with great fits. The seed of an idea was planted in her mind.

And that seed would, after almost a decade and a half, grow into FableStreet, one of India's top domestic brands of Western clothing for Indian ladies. In the interim, Ayushi went on to work at McKinsey & Company as a consultant for six years and then, years later, when she was bitten by the bug of entrepreneurship, she realized that while the need existed, the solution was still not there.

Interestingly, despite her love of well-fitting clothing, Ayushi was never into fashion. A topper in school, she went on to do her engineering from Netaji Subhas University of Technology (NSIT), Delhi (2006) and from there her MBA at Indian Institute of Management Calcutta (IIM Calcutta) (2008) where she was the silver medallist of her batch.

At her campus placement, she was picked up by McKinsey & Company as a consultant and she would stay with McKinsey until 2015, which was when she decided to strike out on her own. It was a huge decision—giving up the security of a position with an internationally reputed firm like McKinsey for the uncertainties and ups and downs that were part and parcel of entrepreneurial life, but she was determined to make it on her own.

In all the years that she had been working as a consultant with McKinsey, she realized she had been picking up workwear whenever she travelled abroad. Her quest for good Western wear in India was still in vain. There was never enough choice in India or abroad and the fits available in India did not work for Indian body shapes which had very specific requirements.

It had been seven years since she had first felt the need, and the gap in this industry still existed. She began exploring the space to determine the feasibility of the idea and, in 2016, FableStreet was born, or FS Life as the company now goes by. The brand began with its own website where customers could order clothes in predetermined sizes as well as custom sizing that was made to fit their unique needs. They then moved into omnichannels by offering their products on online marketplaces like Nykaa, Myntra, Ajio.

They opened their first offline store in 2019 at DLF Promenade, New Delhi, which shut down during the pandemic. Their unique selling point is their in-house Tailored Fit algorithms, which are supported by R&D and guarantee a flawless fit using just three body measures. She personally measured over 200 Indian women to delve deeply into the nuances of Indian sizing and get it right. Today, their database contains the measurements of over a million women. They were the first company in the world to offer a 'my style, your fit' customer solution that serves professional women of all body shapes and sizes.

Back in December 2019, FableStreet raised funding of $3 million in their Series A investment round through Fireside Ventures, followed by another round of funding in 2022. And today, FableStreet is known for the best fits in premium Western wear for Indian women.

Ayushi is immensely fond of travelling, and Isle of Skye in Scotland is her favourite place to visit. As she matured as a traveller, she prefers going to lesser-known destinations rather than the tourist hotspots. Although, one tourist hotspot that she can visit over and over is Paris. She drives, she hikes and she loves music. Other passions include fitness, weightlifting and CrossFit. Whatever she does, comes from a space of passion, whether it is hitting spots off the tourist tracks or keeping herself fit and healthy by working out consistently or whether helping Indian women find the perfect fit for their bodies.

Excerpts from an interview conducted over a call in November 2023:

Tell us about your early years, your family, influences while you were growing up and what did you dream of becoming when you grew up? Although I grew up in what would be regarded as a very typical environment, it was actually rather fascinating in retrospect. A lot of me, of who I am today, is part and parcel of me growing up. I was born and brought up in New Delhi. My father is an ENT specialist, and my mother is a Supreme Court lawyer who has been practising civil law across Delhi NCR. I have a sister who is a year-and-a-half younger to me. Dad always wanted me to do well and set high goals for me and my sister. We were a nuclear family. Dad was busy establishing himself and his practice till the age of 40–45.

We have seen a very independent way of life growing up, and we have also learnt that we have to strive for ourselves because we are not going to get anything on a platter. Our parents raised us in a fairly gender-neutral manner. We were free to pursue our goals and never constrained by our gender. In the sense that if we asked them a reasonable question and they had no logical answer, logic prevailed over culture or sentiment.

We have grown up in a way where everything operated on logic. We weren't compelled to obey something if it couldn't be rationalized. We never had the mindset that our parents would take care of everything for us. They would be busy doing their own thing while encouraging us.

Throughout my time in school, I was a topper and a nerd, and my sister was always called Ayushi's sister. Now that Sakshi has established her own personality, I take delight in being called Sakshi's sister. I think a lot of who I am comes from the fact that our parents enabled us to be independent, and second, they had great expectations for us in terms of who they wanted us to be.

I grew up thinking that I would have to create my life from scratch because I saw them fight for all they have today, and I thought there was no safety net. And they never thought of us as 'daughters' and there was no conversation about when we should get married.

My parents' only focus was on education and on our careers. That shaped my world view of things, so I never grew up believing that there is anything that holds me back. Since I am forty years old, I feel that the argument about feminism and women's lack of representation is unfounded because I grew up with such an unbiased mindset that I could not even see those prejudices.

This made it possible for me to do anything and everything without holding myself back. I have always believed that if I am great at something I will achieve what I want. I have never thought that just because I am a girl I won't be able to do it. As a leader today, I have come to see how common this belief is and how it hinders a lot of women.

Was there any specific reason that made you opt for engineering?
I eliminated the options I did not want to do. When I was a child, the obvious career path for those who excelled academically was either medicine or engineering. I really enjoyed science but I disliked biology, so medical was not an option. Since I enjoyed mathematics, engineering felt like a good choice.

As a child, did fashion and clothes interest you? Were you particular about the way you dressed and did you create your own designs to give to the tailor?
I was always a creative person and there was some element of doing things on my own, building things on my own. There was always a creative component to summer assignments, such as how to make them appear more beautiful. I recall that, in addition to completing my engineering forms, I concurrently filled out the NIFT form because I was drawn to that field and it seemed very exciting. It was not a craze for designing but about learning the elements across creativity, etc. So, there was always a little bit of an inclination.

And as far as the transition to a start-up, I would say what I am doing now feels more natural, even though it is more about business development than creativity. The fashion element was not the driving force behind this. As a professional woman in my early career, I realized the importance of clothing, and how good attire can uplift one's confidence. For me FableStreet is all about making people feel beautiful and confident about themselves, and clothing is one aspect that results in an immediate uptick. When you receive a compliment for dressing well, that makes you feel good about yourself.

After completing your engineering and MBA, you joined McKinsey's consulting team. This was also the time when you realized there was a need for custom-fit, Westernized workwear for Indian women which could be customized. Tell us about this aha moment.

I studied engineering from 2002 to 2006. Women were just starting to enter the professional space which was predominantly a man's world. There were just six women among hundred in my engineering batch. We were only 10 per cent of the entire cohort of IIM Calcutta, today of course, it is 30–40 per cent. Even in McKinsey, there were perhaps two or three women among the 10 people who were hired, that also they got lucky. So that has been the kind of journey, where women have always been in the minority in the professional space. Coming back to Western wear, the entire idea or challenge started when I had to appear for my summer placement interviews.

Because I was a large size, I would never really get clothes that would fit me. It was customary for tailors to visit the campus and sew suits for the men. But when I had to return to Delhi for my summer internship in 2006, I had no choice but to purchase a jacket and trousers from the only store that offered them in a poor-quality fabric out of all the offline stores that existed at the time. Today if I look at it, I would never dream of wearing it. They had such limited sizing that the largest size was just large and did not fit me. It was such a sorry state of affairs.

But I pretty much stuffed myself into it and appeared for my summer placements and got through. I went to the US, bought a lot of stuff from there. I joined McKinsey when I finished B-School. The issue of not finding great Western workwear for women persisted for seven to eight years. I would still have trouble finding nice clothes. I would just buy clothes abroad or pick up from select international brands because nobody was making clothing that would fit Indian women's bodies.

Our sizes are very different from Western sizes. And it was surprising that no one had tried to solve it. I had identified the issues in 2006 and even 10 years later no one had invested energy and time and tried to resolve these. And then I decided to explore this idea. Does it make sense to explore well-fitting Western wear in India? Back then, I thought of workwear because that was what I was associated with. I began exploring the concept at two levels. One, there was a business opportunity and two I always wanted to do something which drives large-scale impact and builds a business.

After spending some time talking to people and conducting surveys, I came to the conclusion that women were still struggling to locate appropriate need-based clothing, while the world was shifting towards a Western fashion style.

India has a big market and a thriving apparel sector. International brands have also relied on India for their supplies. One could create a multimillion-dollar brand coming out of India because there were no restrictions on market opportunities. Given that I had experienced that difficulty as a customer, it was intriguing to see how a fantastic business opportunity intersected with an area that I could identify with. I jumped in and said, 'Hey, let's do it.' Because everything coincided well, it made sense to start it, and so FableStreet's journey began.

How did you train yourself in this completely new field, given you came from a corporate background? How did you set about translating this idea into an enterprise?

I always believe that you have to get your hands dirty and learn. McKinsey builds interesting mindsets in you and one of the things you learn is to drive large-scale impact. Which is why I was always dreaming big. By virtue of being a consultant, I had gone through the process of immersing rapidly in a sector, learning about it in a very short time, at a very quick pace, and then delving deep into it. That enabled me to go right in with the belief that I could succeed and that I could fast learn the specifics of the industry and the sector.

Having said that, the process of execution is still quite challenging, you still have to put in some training. In light of this, I actually spent a year in the pre-development stage, learning every facet of the garment business, including design, women's sizing, garment manufacture, and the intricacy of the processes. I created a one-page strategy for FableStreet in 2016, and that is still in place today.

Thus, learning the aspects of the business, from the ground up, getting inventory, getting the product right—all these were important. Once you get into it, you have to go through the process and learn the technicalities. Since we were starting from scratch, I pretty much interned and worked at export houses, learning every facet of the business from procurement to design, fitting, sizing and a lot of analyticals on sizing. I wanted to resolve operational complexities in order to deliver my vision.

How did you come up with the name FableStreet?

We were going through a number of names, and for me, the name had to be international, and it had to be meaningful to who I was, and what I was building as a well-fitted workwear brand with an international look and feel. We went through a lot of permutations and combinations and many of them were just not available. FableStreet was one of the names that we surveyed and tested among our target consumers.

Making professional women feel good about themselves while acknowledging that every woman is different, deserves her own space, and can write her own story was one of my goals while I was creating this. Fable being story and street being linked to shopping streets, so it fit. In the early days, we used the tagline, 'Tailor your story'. We don't use it any more.

Tell us about the tailored-to-fit algorithm that you developed. What went into the creation of it and how was it a game changer for FableStreet?

When I began in 2016, I personally measured over 200-odd women to know how it works. I had all the international size charts and Indian size charts and so I believe I learnt a lot about unique characteristics of Indian bodies, which made me understand how to convert these insights into the right fitted garment. The majority of Western clothing that is sold here is based on size charts from the US and the UK. All brands have just copy pasted that sizing and brought those patterns and cuts to India in the same shapes and sizes.

Many of those garments are made for 5-foot-8-inch tall European women who have very different body structures. Whereas for Indian women, the average height even in metros is 5 foot 4 inch or lower, and the majority of Indian women are pear shaped—there is more volume on the chest and the hip area. In the age group that I am now, most of us will have a paunch because one has grown up in a different environment where exercising was not the norm.

When you go into the specifics of garment construction, you need to understand that it has to be different for Indian women. The chest and hip areas have to be more voluminous. You can't copy paste a European pattern and say this will really fit you. Even if it is the right size, the constructions are very different from what we need for our body types.

Secondly, when I was growing up, if you were shorter, and you saw someone taller wearing something you wanted to wear, the first thought was to cut the length of the garment. Once you go into the technicalities of understanding body sizing and choosing the right size, you realize that technically if you are shorter, all your body parts and proportions are also shorter.

You cannot say, 'I'll cut the garment at the bottom and it will fit me', if you require a good fit since your arms and torso are shorter, your shoulder-to-chest maximum peak point is lower, and the distance between your shoulder and waist is shorter. Everything needs to be changed, including your waist and chest points. If you want to acquire Indian fits correctly, you must first be data-centric and learn about the Indian body size chart. Then, you must make the garment match the

Indian size chart by adjusting the details. Therefore, you must create an entirely new set of pattern banks.

All this is just in terms of solving fits, applying only to fitting problems. Then there is the question of finding solutions for Indian women in terms of our workplace culture, stylistic sensibility and content. Our country has a humid, tropical environment all year round so you really can't have heavy fabrics and polyester.

Back in 2016, Western fashion sensibilities were just beginning to emerge in India. You couldn't have thigh length, above knee length and sleeveless. Today there is a very different sensibility, it has evolved. The culture of copying designs and stitching new clothes is on the decline.

How does a typical day look like for you and how do you relax?
My typical day is actually very unstructured, but I am trying to make it better organized. But the kind of start-up and the set up that I am in, you know you arrive with a plan to accomplish this and then something or the other goes wrong, causing your day to go for a toss, and you end up doing something completely different from what you had planned.

That happens on a lot of days but if I were to take a step back and think of how I usually end up structuring my day and look at the day, I would say from a work perspective I spend around 30 to 40 per cent of my time on business, on direct deliverables and goals, and another 30 to 40 per cent of the time that I need to do to finish off my to-dos. The remaining 20 to 30 per cent of my time is spent with the team, engaging with them and understanding them, problem solving, etc. That's what I do from a work perspective. I love spending time with my family and watching my son grow up every day. So, I lead a very simple life, but that's how my day looks like.

What are your future plans?

We are planning to open 25 offline stores. Also, we are aiming to grow more brands like Pink Fort. The next few years are going to be super exciting!

What advice would you give women who are considering pursuing entrepreneurship?

The first advice I would say is that very often gender bias arises in our minds. So at least in your own head you have to think of yourself as an entrepreneur and not a woman entrepreneur. You must begin by believing that you are just as good as your counterpart, and I believe that changing one's perspective is the most important thing anyone can do. In my head, I have never ever thought of gender as a factor in being an entrepreneur and that is why I am where I am.

And the second is, in terms of planning, execution and fundraising, I would say think big, start small and execute fast. That is the best way to operate and run any kind of business.

Lastly, I would advise you to approach business development holistically and with great consideration, paying close attention to the numbers you are examining.

6

"Entrepreneurs are actually trying to solve problems that will benefit millions of people"

Naiyya Saggi
Founder, Edition;
Group Co-Founder, The Good Glamm Group;
Founder, BabyChakra

Naiyya Saggi had no idea of what she was going to do with her life as a young girl, growing up in West Bengal where her mother, an IAS officer, was posted. Her mother had instilled in Naiyya and her elder sister Nadia early on that work and life were intertwined—their dinner-time conversations were centred around her work, and young Naiyya often studied in her mother's office after school hours. She saw early on the importance of women being in the workforce, being passionately committed to their work and managing home and work with equal ease. Naiyya knew that she would be a woman with a career. Though she wasn't quite clear about what that career would be.

Her academic record wasn't exactly stellar; her parents worried about her, as most parents are wont to do. When Nadia got into the National Law School (NLS) in Bengaluru, as a younger sibling who unquestioningly followed the footsteps of her elder sister, Naiyya decided to study there too. However, it wasn't as easy as it sounds; there was a very tough entrance exam to clear, which Naiyya passed easily.

Perhaps, the most pivotal years of her life were those she spent at NLS. It gave her the opportunity to intern with organizations like Pratham, the Iraqi Special Tribunal at the International Bar Association, London, as well as with legal luminaries like the former Chief Justice of India K.G. Balakrishnan. It was at the NLS that she found her wings, so to speak.

At Pratham, an NGO, she worked with slum children and women. Perhaps at this point, a seed was planted in her mind that whatever she ended up doing, it would have to benefit women and children. After law school, she joined McKinsey as a management consultant where she worked in the space of scaling healthcare, ITES companies and education, and then studied at Harvard Business School (HBS) as a Fulbright and Tata scholar.

She joined the Bridgespan Group (Boston) after graduating from Harvard. Her husband was working with McKinsey at Boston, when one fine day Naiyya decided to return to India and become part of the Indian growth story. She wanted to become an entrepreneur.

And so, within a couple of months, the couple upped and booked one-way tickets to Mumbai. It wasn't easy, it took a huge leap of faith to upend a comfortable life in the United States and move back to India where they had to begin all over again, but Naiyya was determined. It was where things were happening and this was where she had to be if she was to be part of the digital revolution sweeping the country.

When she returned, Naiyya had many conversations with a lot of IT professionals and entrepreneurs, trying to crystallize her plans as to what she should actually do. She spoke with those who had built verticals and scaled them up. Deep down Naiyya knew that her future work would focus on maternal and child health and well-being. She had worked with the Gates Foundation while at McKinsey, and was familiar with it.

It was around this time, Nadia had a baby and Naiyya would spend hours searching the internet for resources and information about India with little luck. Naiyya saw an opportunity here and was eager to grab it. It was around this time, that she reconnected with an old friend, Mitesh Karia. He was in finance and investing and they decided to join hands to build BabyChakra. To get a sense of what mothers wanted and were looking for, they first went to the market and spoke with around 1,200 moms. They realized that the mother and child industry was ripe for disruption in the digital space. In December 2014, they launched BabyChakra.

At this point, Naiyya was not a mother herself, which added to the challenges. Mitesh would eventually move on from BabyChakra, and Naiyya continued on her own as the sole owner.

Naiyya soon managed to find early investors, including the Singapore Angel Network, the Mumbai Angels consortium, and leading individual angels from India and the US. But the journey to raise funds didn't come without the experiences that define how women entrepreneurs were still perceived. In fact, in one of the initial angel investor meetings, she was asked what would happen when she got pregnant and started a family.

She walked out of the meeting, appalled that this reductive question had been asked of her, and all her credentials and expertise had not been considered.

In another incident, she attended an investor pitch meeting when she was nine months' pregnant and was told to come back in three months, when she was more ready to handle things. This incident too left her visibly annoyed. She worked till the day before she had her baby and was back in the office barely two weeks after her baby was born.

With a mothers' community of over 25 million members and a doctor network of 10,000, BabyChakra quickly rose to prominence as one of the top forums and websites for mothers to access knowledge and resources. At this point, the founder of MyGlamm, one of India's largest colour cosmetics brands, Darpan Sanghvi, asked her to come on board as a co-founder and president leading the mother-child vertical with their acquisition of BabyChakra, and she accepted. Darpan, Priyanka Gill and Naiyya then went on to form The Good Glamm Group.

With a valuation of $1.2 billion, the Good Glamm Group became South Asia's largest digital first FMCG conglomerate, acquired multiple popular content and D2C brands and broke into the unicorn club after raising $150 million in their Series D funding led by Prosus Ventures, Warburg Pincus and others. After three years of development, motivated by the goal of creating a cutting-edge Indian consumer electronics brand for the global market, Naiyya left the organization after vesting her shares. She recently launched Edition along with a global founding team.

Excerpts from an interview conducted in Mumbai, in August 2023.

Tell us a bit about your childhood, your growing years, and what dreams and ambitions did you have for yourself?

I grew up in a household where, even in the 1980s, I was fortunate to see my parents enjoying an equal relationship. You don't realize that when you are a child, but later, as you grow up, and become part of these conversations on gender equality, you understand how special and unique that was at the time. My parents were partners on an extremely equal footing. My mum has always been a major force in my life.

She was a Punjabi raised in Amritsar. She got into the services when she was very young, moved to Bengal because she was allotted the West Bengal cadre, picked up Bengali, lived in districts, and gained experience dealing with riots, custodial rapes, managing politicians and all sorts of stakeholders. She has been a huge source of inspiration to me personally. Since we were growing up in Kolkata, our dinner table conversations were not only intense, but also highly intellectual and political. On top of that, my parents encouraged us to lead a life where we could impact and contribute to the society.

My sister, Nadia, who is four years older than me, is a strong-willed personality. Growing up, neither of us never felt that we were any different from the boys in our neighbourhood or social circles; we were equals.

With the exception of the periods when my mother was a DM or assigned to the Governor of Bengal, where we lived in the Raj Bhavan or the DM's home in the district—typically a huge British-style bungalow with a surprise (usually snakes) around every corner—we used to spend our time in government colonies. The government flats, as you know, are fairly basic and far from luxurious. However, what was really magnificent back then, and I realize it more so now, was that we developed a sense of community while growing up.

Everyone knew everybody in these apartments and was enough and more space for the kids to play. The flats were built on large plots of land, so there was enough space to play badminton, race, run around and play hide-and-seek with the neighbourhood kids. This contributed to building a great sense of community. In fact, some of my closest friends are from those days.

I studied at La Martiniere and I was a terrible student. I want to say this loud and clear so because I don't want the bad students to lose hope.

You studied law at the National Law School, even interned with some legal luminaries, and then went on to become an entrepreneur. Did entrepreneurship even enter your mind as a future career when you were a child?

Growing up in West Bengal, the word *dhandaa* or business was used derogatively. Frankly, even in my family, businessmen were looked down upon because of their improper ways of generating wealth or value. Although I was raised in a culture that did not encourage discussion on entrepreneurship, it is fascinating to note that my *nani* was an entrepreneur.

She got married to my *nana* when she was very young, as was customary for women those days. My nana insisted on her completing her graduation and she even did her B. Ed back then. My nana retired from the army fairly early and he went to Saudi Arabia to pick up a job there. And my nani was left behind with three daughters and she desperately needed to earn some money because he wasn't earning quite enough to support his family, and still have enough left over to save for their weddings.

She went to a nearby school and asked the principal for a teaching position. Apparently, that lady said, 'No, I don't want to hire your kind, I want a fancier-looking teacher.' That prompted my nani to say, 'To hell with you,' and she founded her own school, making it one of the largest schools in Amritsar at one point in time.

It was important for my grandmother to prove to the principal that it is not always about being fancy but also about being a woman of substance. I think we learnt to respect entrepreneurship from her, but we never really saw it as a viable option though we admired her work immensely. That was the closest brush I had with entrepreneurship, and then there was the law school, NLS, which was far removed from entrepreneurship. All my internships were either with the Chief Justice of India or with the International Bar Association, which entailed a lot of humanitarian law work. Right after law school, McKinsey happened. It was here that I had my first brush with business, of actually seeing business at scale and seeing the impact it can have.

Tell us about your years at NLS and what were your takeaways that still stand you in good stead?

At NLS, the one story that was very formative for me had nothing to do with business but more to do with building my personal reservoir of strength, and learning what it should be. For the first three years at the law school, the environment was fantastic with talented and driven kids. I felt very much at home there. I was my class representative for many years, with a large group of friends, and then I decided to stand for university president. This was a time when there were not very many women who had been university president.

So, I thought, fine, let me stand for the post. I wasn't trying to make a feminist point, I seriously thought that I could do something different for the student body. I loved the feeling of being responsible for outcomes. At that time, I had got a lot of messages from people discouraging me from contesting the election because of my gender. This was in 2005. I recall this was the first time in my life that I ever had to deal with a gender-related issue.

I don't know why they thought that I couldn't handle a leadership role because I was a woman. It was nasty and my mobile phone was buzzing at 2 or 3 in the morning with people yelling, 'Stand down, stand down.' I had people yelling me down even when I was giving my election speech, it was really unpleasant. And I won.

I remember feeling lonely when the votes were being counted; I had only one or two friends with me, who reassured me that I did the right thing when I won. Even though I was under a lot of peer pressure, I think it was a powerful moment for me because it taught me that sometimes it is all right to make a choice that makes you less popular in a given situation. You have to stand for what is right for you and choose the correct course of action. I became the third female president.

I am particularly proud of the fact that following my term, women presidents began to be elected almost every alternate year. Perhaps the students observed the excellent work done by them. I believe I learned a lot from that experience, which may have been my first leadership role.

You bagged a Fulbright and Tata scholarship to Harvard, and then you worked at the Bridgespan Group (Boston) and McKinsey in the space of maternal and child health and education. What drove your decision to come back to India?

It wasn't a lengthy discussion between Sandeep and I when we discussed returning to our country. We were married then. I kept on reading about all the wonderful things that were happening in India, and I would eagerly keep reading the YourStory articles about entrepreneurs and how everyone now had a cell phone. And I thought to myself, *If I am not part of this today, I will get left behind.* I was determined to be part of this wave even if it meant moving back to India.

Of course, life was extremely comfortable in the US, in the sense that it is almost predictable, but life in India was so unpredictable. Even though it was home it was so uncertain, and that is where some of us thrive when we embrace it. I literally sat down my husband one Sunday evening, and said, 'I'm done, we're going back to India.' He replied, 'Okay sure. When? Within six months, ten months, or next year?' I replied, 'Next week.'

Sandeep was all practical about it, saying, 'Let our leaves finish.' I asked, 'How many months do we have? He replied, 'We have three.' I said, 'Well then, we'll relinquish the two months and get back in a month.' We flipped a coin because we couldn't decide between Bengaluru and Mumbai. I believed that I needed to work in a city that had an entrepreneurial culture of some kind so that I could work crazy long hours without fear.

It turned out to be Mumbai, and we booked one-way tickets to the city. Sandeep had just moved to McKinsey in Boston, telling everyone his future was in healthcare at the Boston office. And within a year, he was essentially telling everyone that he was moving back to India because his future was in the Mumbai office. I say this all the time that life is a partnership and the cooperation of your spouse is extremely important, and mine deserves all the credit for that. It is the greatest investment you will ever make for your career and overall happiness.

How did entrepreneurship come to you? Specifically, the idea of BabyChakra came to you after you saw your sister struggling with being a new mom, but how did you identify that there was a wider need for something like this and then build it?

I had worked on maternal and child health while I was at McKinsey, so the concept of BabyChakra had been with me for a while. I was a member of the Gates Foundation team that was developing the entire maternal and child health strategy for India. I was required to visit rural areas, interact with people in PHCs, meet *anganwadi* and Asha workers, and understand how the Integrated Child Development Services (ICDS) Scheme, the Ministry of Health and Family Welfare and the Ministry of Women and Child Development work.

The more I went to the ground, in areas where the projects were more successful, I learnt that what worked was when women, I mean mothers came together and shared their experiences in a non-judgemental and safe space with a strong sense of community. There were healthcare workers who were intervening at the right time, in the right way and with the right intent. That sense of offline community always stayed with me. In those conversations, I also learnt that the mother-in-law, the father and the overall community played a significant role in the success of the healthcare, wellness and nutrition outcomes of the women and children. Then, when I was at Harvard Business School, some amazing digital products had just launched. Both Uber and

Instagram were recently launched. I think we called one of the first Ubers at Cambridge because we wanted to see how it worked.

It was like magic. Wonderful digital products were being developed to meet basic human needs: transportation, connections, food and even to find love. I was left wondering, *How do you create a supportive ecosystem and knowledge for families, not just mothers, through pregnancy and parenting?* When I moved back to India, I was quite convinced I would do something like BabyChakra. I did explore other things, of course.

I spoke with individuals in the start-up space; for example, I met Rahul Yadav of Housing.com and Bhavish Aggarwal of Ola. I was asked by a lot of folks whether I wanted to take on leadership roles in their companies. While I loved the conversations, I was determined to do something on my own. And the idea of BabyChakra stuck with me, I mean the name wasn't there at the time, but just the idea of how I wanted to create a platform that supports mothers at a crucial phase in their lives in a hyper-personalized, safe and non-judgemental way.

You began with BabyChakra. This was a platform for mothers. At the point, you yourself were not a mother. Did you feel a shift when you eventually became a mom, in terms of how you yourself related to the brand?

I never felt at that point that not being a mother myself was a limitation. Of course, today in hindsight as a mother myself, I realize that how it could have really helped me. However, it helped me feel more objective and prevented me from bringing my unconscious biases and ideas about how a solution should be presented. Entrepreneurs are actually trying to solve problems that will benefit millions of people.

To make that real, they need to first listen to the individuals whose problems they are attempting to solve. Many a time, we get so stuck up in thinking that we know the answer because we have the problem, that we get blind to the real solutions, so I think it was helpful for me to have the objectivity. My familiarity with the industry was also beneficial. Because I had experience working in the medical field and, more significantly, because I was listening a lot, I was able to speak the lingo from a healthcare standpoint.

I was picking up lingo even on social media, such as EBF (exclusively breastfeeding), MIL (mother-in-law), OCO (one child only) because I was listening so intently, and that gave me a sense of belonging even though I wasn't a mother myself at the time. You know, all of these lingos that mothers use are almost like a secret code among them.

What difficulties did you encounter as a female entrepreneur? How easy or difficult was it to build the platform, get funding in a space that was increasingly getting crowded? What would you tell entrepreneurs looking to start in their fundraising journey?

My co-founder had to leave in the very first year when we started because he got married and we did not have any money. Obviously, it was difficult. He was a childhood friend, and we are best friends even today. It was not easy, but he moved on. So, at that point I had to make a decision—do I move forward or take a step back and close. I chose to move forward every single time, more out of insane optimism. It seems to work because if you believe in something, you will attract believers who believe in you.

You have to look for them, but when you find them hold them close. Even in fundraising, I have had similar conversations. Naturally,

I have had these conversations early, like what happens when I will get pregnant or if I could bring in someone to explain the P&L to me. I had to remind some people that I had an MBA degree from Harvard so I knew what I am talking about. In the process, the investors I have found have been amazing.

It was difficult because I had to deal with lawyers and different stakeholders during the decision-making process that would decide BabyChakra's future, including whether we would use internal or external funding or merge.

I remember that Karan Maheshwari, one of my investors, would call me at 8 every morning to see how I was doing and not ask about the company or the holdings.

The other investors like Arihant Patni, Anand Chandrashekharan, Maninder Gulati, Arun Nanda would also keep checking on me to see how I was doing and guiding me especially in my lowest moments. They had my back unquestionably.

I want to just leave the message behind that as an entrepreneur who happens to be a woman, it is not just about you pitching to the investors, it is also about them pitching to you because you have to find the right partner to watch out for you when things get tough. So, all I want to say is, don't be in a hurry to close with people who don't respect you. You are your gender and it is totally okay because it is totally you and it is part of your strength. I do a bunch of angel checks now.

I tell all entrepreneurs, not just women, that nothing succeeds like success. So, keep on building your company, even if you are bootstrapping or even just raising a seed funding round. When you start making money, or start creating an impact people start reaching out to you. And then you are able to negotiate terms, negotiate a deal and that is a critical and a powerful position to be in. Try to hold off fundraising too as much as possible, for as long as possible, if you can, if you are able to scale. As long as bootstrapping is leading to growth; but if you are just wallowing along, it doesn't make sense.

If your company needs the investment in order to fuel growth, you should not shy away from seeking it. Don't make bootstrapping the easy way out.

Who would you call your mentors and what are the lessons you've learnt from them?

I learn a lot from conversations. I am currently doing the Mompreneur podcast, and there are so many things I have learnt from these conversations. For example, Neelu Khatri, co-founder, Akasa Air, spoke at length about the critics versus the promoters, emphasizing that we need to focus on the latter more. And I think that is such an important observation because that is how I have lived my life, but I have never really been able to articulate it with as much clarity as she did in that conversation with me.

Or, for instance, Arti Gill, who sold Oziva to Unilever. She built the business from scratch, brought on a co-founder in the middle. We talked about how she found the confidence in herself to go out and conduct her fundraising conversations because the company's success spoke for itself. Sometimes it is just good to focus, create and construct and then let your work do the talking. I think these were the discussions that really helped me grasp what was happening around me as well. While HBS did teach us case studies of entrepreneurship, when it came to applying it to one's own entrepreneurial journey the learnings are very different.

Talking to the amazing Faye D'Souza also gave an interesting perspective on life. She spoke about a time when she left *Mirror Now* and how it was one of the lowest moments of her life, and then how she chose to not put a full stop but instead, a pause or a comma to her career to become a parent. She has since started her own venture, Beatroot Media. All these conversations teach you so much about how people live their lives, and then you take what you want from it.

Tell us how the acquisition by the Good Glamm Group came about, how did you align yourself with your other co-founders?
This is interestingly captured in an HBS case study, which coincidentally was written by my entrepreneurship professor. This was 2020, in the beginning when COVID hit, and I had two term sheets—we were negotiating shareholders' agreements (SHAs) in one, and suddenly both term sheets were withdrawn because of the pandemic and no one knew what was happening. I clearly remember the day when I heard about the term sheets and the SHAs being withdrawn. I literally collapsed when I got that phone call.

Practically, I knew why that would happen given the uncertainties with COVID, but at that point in time it felt like why me. We had only six months of money left in the bank. We have two options, I thought at the time: we can continue the way we are and be frugal or we shut shop. We went the first way and we did really well. We cut our costs, everyone took a salary cut to support the company through, we made every penny count, we launched three products right at the start of the pandemic which became BabyChakra private label products—it came together beautifully.

It was always my dream to have BabyChakra products. We have always said, *'Har ghar BabyChakra',* and we have demonstrated that with digital technology. Now we were doing this with products we had co-created with mothers and doctors. We launched on Amazon because we didn't have our own warehouses and the products did so well that after three days Amazon blocked us, claiming that there must be some sort of scam going on because it was impossible for six months' worth of products to run out of stock in a month without paid marketing or Amazon ads.

I remember I was sitting with my chief of marketing, Anvita, and our phones were going *tik tik tik tik* because literally every second there was a product being bought. We were doing fairly well, but we were still at the position where we needed to consider raising capital. Our internal team came together and said we are happy to put in another round, and we had an American investor who was happy to invest too, so that was one term sheet that came my way in 2021. Meanwhile, Darpan Sanghvi, the founder of MyGlamm, reached out to me.

It was actually the third time he had reached out. In fact, the first two times, we had not met. We finally met at his house, both of us with our masks on because of the pandemic. But my mask came off pretty soon because I like to see people. He said to me that the dream we have is aligned and it made sense to me when he explained it to me in person. He asked, 'How do we create a digital-first conglomerate of the future?

He then added, 'How do we expand this further, given the resources we have at BabyChakra, PopXO and our future assets, as well as the fact that MyGlamm is a product firm and BabyChakra is a very powerful brand? I want you to join me as a co-founder because this is a long-term vision that I want to build.'

Priyanka Gill from PopXO had just joined him as co-founder. Do keep in mind that I was a single founder and had built BabyChakra on my own.

By then, I had gone through the entire journey of fundraising, building the entire company, the team and the products on my own. While it was great, it does get exhausting and you want to build with positive people. So, I went back to my shareholders and said, 'Hey, we have two options before us', and to their credit they said, 'Naiyya, we leave it up to you.'

It was really a powerful statement for me and I felt so relieved that they trusted me with such an important decision.

From being bootstrapped, to being funded and now you are yourself an angel investor. What have been your learnings?
Nothing has changed. I mean, entrepreneurship and investment is a people game. As an angel, you are betting on the team, the people, the founders very early on. Another thing I have learnt is that people's intrinsic value systems remain the same. The businesses I have made investments in are doing very well, and companies that consistently do well are run by entrepreneurs who have a set of principles that have been constant over time, such as being transparent, being ethical, being team-oriented and customer-focused.

The second thing I believe I have learnt is that market timing is super critical; there are times when you are too ahead for the market. Don't try to fight it, just get out of it if you need to for a while. I genuinely believe in this. Sometimes it is good to be a second mover too. Honestly, I don't believe in this first-mover advantage. Why are you wasting all that money establishing the market, let someone else do that and learn from their experience. There is value in being a second mover in a developing market, with bricks already being set by an earlier competitor and then moving in really fast and blitz scaling it.

You are passionate about women in technology. What do you do to encourage, mentor, build women in this space? What can society do to help?

This is something I am really passionate about. I'll talk about three pivotal moments that were really important to me personally. I remember saying, 'There are no women in this week's pipeline', when looking at the deal flow pipeline on a call with a group of angel investors I co-advise. They were like, 'Yeah, because there are very few women entrepreneurs.' Even though I don't get upset very often, that statement infuriated me.

That made me determined to show everybody that I won't bring them five, ten, fifteen, I'll bring you hundred women entrepreneurs. That is when I got in touch with SK, the editor of *Mint,* with Aastha who leads Startup India, Abha from Ladies Who Lead, and basically told everybody that we should create the definitive list of 100 incredible women who are building India and that we should change the narrative.

In fact, that was a special moment for me because within a week we were all working around the clock to ensure that women's entrepreneurship day, which nobody really cared about, is celebrated on a grand scale. Since it fell on a Saturday, a week from then, we decided to use that to launch. Everyone said we were crazy, and that it seemed impossible to obtain 100 names and bios, and perform the kind of quality checks required by print.

We said that was our task to make the impossible possible and to leave it to us. The team worked 24x7 those seven days. We accepted nominations, self-nominations, and 1,200 nominations were received. We had to choose 100 of them so we selected 100, and wrote out their bios. The editor of *Mint* had promised that he would link the article to the paper's digital edition too. But he was so inspired by it, that the night before he said, 'I'm going to give you four pages in the main edition.' I was shocked, and pleasantly surprised, this has never happened before.

We got four pages in *Mint*. I think that it was for the first time that 100 women entrepreneurs were profiled in a mainstream financial national daily. That article went viral, and the best part was that it was not just women sharing it, many men, including the likes of Piyush Goyal, talked about it. That report became one of the most popular articles that *Mint* ever published in 2022. I believe that stating, 'Let's just get the stories together and get the stories out', was a turning point in my life.

The second is this whole series that I am doing on mompreneurs, which is an extension of that. You see, there is a segment of women leaders who have built big businesses, such as Anita Dongre, Falguni Nayar, Namita Thapar, Lizzie Chapman, Faye D'Souza, Aarti Gill. But we also have another segment where we have mom microentrepreneurs. So get their stories out, get funding and, most importantly, get them to earn the respect and the recognition they deserve. They are the backbone of our economy and are highly valued in our local communities and society. We rely on them to provide daycare and tiffin services, etc.

We are taking this initiative. The whole idea is that at the end of it, the top three winners will receive seed money from the group at the end of the competition as well as advice from the jury members and mentorship from the who's who of India. And of course, there is the partnership with FICCI FLO (FICCI Ladies Organisation), Startup India and Aspire for Her. That is the other thing I am extremely proud of, and as part of this, I am getting out the stories of successful entrepreneurs who are also moms to encourage others that this can be done. Finally, I have been a mentor with Google and Facebook, and I started my angel investments, which give me a lot of joy.

I have a soft corner for women in tech building tech products, so, these three things are pivotal to how I can support this community.

What does Naiyya Saggi's day look like?
I drink a lot of coffee. [*And she laughs.*] I wake up early in the morning and spend time with my daughters, especially the older one before she rushes off to school, and then hit the gym. I try to go to the gym a little more frequently these days, as it gives me a lot of mental clarity. I try to find some alone time in the course of the day. I think the older I am growing, I am becoming a little more introverted, and I am kind of enjoying it. I love spending time with my husband, we have a lot of conversations and quiet time.

We listen to music and read. I love art, my mother has been an influence there. When I was growing up, she used to have a lot of artists come over at home—Manjit Bawa was one of them. He had created these two sketches which are framed and kept for posterity in my house. I have grown really passionate about art over the years, especially about the work by up-and-coming artists. I can't say I am a collector but I do have a few pieces at home that I am extremely proud of, which I will treasure and pass on to my daughters.

7

"[W]omen must be aware of this imposter syndrome and be confident about their abilities"

Namrata Asthana
Co-Founder,
Blue Tokai

Hers is definitely an unusual career trajectory. Growing up in Muscat, Namrata Asthana lived the expat experience as part of a large Indian community. She moved to the US to study at Vanderbilt University with a major in psychology and a minor in anthropology. She also studied for the associate of arts (AA) digital communication and multimedia from The Art Institute, Chicago. In 2002, she moved to India.

Namrata first worked with the American India Foundation and then PepsiCo India and the Centre of Development Finance at the Institute of Finance Management and Research (IFMR) near Chennai. She also worked with Alliance India. Coffee figured absolutely nowhere in this story, except perhaps as a beverage that got her through her day. But that was all destined to change. She had also, within this span, met and married Matt Chitharanjan, a graduate from NYU Stern School of Business. He had moved to India in 2011 to work on SME (small and medium enterprise) access to finance research with IFMR and was in Chennai on work.

After they were married, they moved to New Delhi where they both had the idea to launch a coffee business that procured its beans ethically. That was when the idea for Blue Tokai Coffee Roasters was born. It was something that began completely on a whim. They had no background in the coffee business except for a love for coffee. They started from scratch— googling up coffee estates on the Coffee Board website, cold calling, emailing them all and waiting for them to reply.

Serendipitously, all the estates they wrote to responded and even entertained them, regardless of the fact that what they were asking for were minuscule quantities of coffee compared with the regular quantities they were accustomed to in the orders they received. In order to obtain the volumes required for the online orders they were receiving, they began in 2013 with a one-kg equipment that they used to roast beans for 12 to 14 hours.

Namrata put her graphic design skills to use and designed the logo, the word tokai came from an old Malabar word for the plume of the peacock, a bird which is often seen in coffee estates. Starting as an online delivery roast-on-demand service for coffee beans, they sent across their specialty coffees to coffee enthusiasts across the country. Since then, they have improved both their equipment and their location, which was just two rooms on the terrace of Namrata's parents' Gurugram home when they started.

It has been a long, arduous and completely unexpected pivot into entrepreneurship for both of them. They visited estates, sampled coffee, observed how coffee was grown and harvested, and learnt about the business hitting the ground running. They bought a roaster with their savings and took online orders for freshly roasted coffee. As the word spread, they began getting orders from across the country. They went on to open their first offline cafe and store in the Saidulajab area of New Delhi and today have cafes all across the country.

Their coffee is monitored by a Q-Grade certified director of coffee, and roasted in their units spread in Gurugram and Bengaluru. They have over 80 outlets in cities like Kolkata, Delhi, Mumbai and Gurugram. Their packaged roasted coffee beans and canned coffee are available on online platforms as well as their own site. While Namrata handles the design and brand experience part of the business, Matt looks after the financial aspect.

They were eventually joined by Shivam Sahi as a co-founder who is now the COO of the business. According to *Business Today*, they raised $30 million in their Series B funding which was led by A 91 Partners.

Namrata set about on a completely different trajectory of life, moving from the corporate world to setting up a business that would redefine how India looked at consuming coffee in homes. Blue Tokai is now a familiar name to people who appreciate fine indigenous coffees in the country. For Namrata, the journey has been tough but fun—building a brand, spreading awareness about coffee and using her platform to create space for wider, important conversations.

Excerpts from the interview conducted over email in 2023:

Tell us a bit about your childhood, your family, your growing years. What you were as a child and what were your ambitions for yourself back then, if any?
I grew up in Muscat and then went to the US. But while we were in Oman, Dad started his first company in our house with one of the

rooms as his office. In the beginning, there were just two people in his company. In retrospect, this seems so ironic because I really do believe that it set the path for us to start our own company. We started Blue Tokai in a room at my parents' house. For me it didn't seem unusual, it might be because I have grown up in that environment.

As a child I was always interested in how people lived and thought, which is why I studied psychology and anthropology at Vanderbilt. I do feel that all the communication that I do, all the customer interface, seeing the things you do, how do you make the workplace a better place to be, how do you enhance the customer experience, I think it all stemmed from my childhood and my growing years.

You graduated from Vanderbilt University with a major in psychology and a minor in anthropology. Then you worked in design, in the social sector, in corporate communications in the US and then in Delhi. This is a rather unconventional career graph. What made you pursue psychology and anthropology and then move to design and corporate communications? What made you return to India? Psychology and anthropology for me were intertwined because I was always intrigued by the culture of Oman—how people thought, their language and their way of living. And whenever we visited India during summers, I was fascinated by the culture here when I was young and even now. I think that also played a role in me moving back to India.

Communication has always been important to me, hence I had a keen interest in exploring how we communicate with each other as a culture and how we communicate our needs. I remember there was no English TV when we were growing up, so my best friend and I would watch these Arabic shows and we would make up stories about what they were saying in our heads. That was our connection there. A lot of it stemmed from our fascination about culture and how people express themselves.

What made Matt and you launch Blue Tokai?

When I moved to Chennai for a year, I loved the small kiosks where you could get freshly ground coffee, or if you brought the coffee beans with you, they could grind it for you. There was some interaction with coffee. There were coffee shops everywhere, but you had no idea where it was coming from and it was most likely a combination of chicory and Robusta, which was not what we wanted to do.

And when we moved to Delhi, whenever I went to get coffee from the bigger coffee chains and I asked them where it was from, they were unable to provide any information. I remember Matt and I were staying in our little barsati then doing different jobs, when one fine day I said, 'I just want someone to deliver a freshly brewed cup of coffee for me and I should know which estate it was from.'

Matt and I were working at different jobs at the time. I used to have a lot of these ideas and Matt paid no heed to them, he would laugh them off, but this time he said, 'You know we could actually do that, it is not a bad idea', which is how it all started.

And so, we began cold calling all these coffee companies and no one got back to us, and I thought, we don't know anybody in the coffee industry, we haven't grown up here, so maybe it would be a little bit harder than it would be for other people. But then in the email we had mentioned that we would be coming to Bengaluru on a certain date.

What we did not know was that they would have their own calendars, so they set up all the emails they get from buyers there. Then, when the time comes for them to sell their coffee, they begin phoning the buyers. So, a week before we were supposed to reach Bengaluru, all the people we had emailed called us back. They were just so warm and friendly. They hosted us, they talked to us, they invited us to their offices, even though we were two strangers who were asking for such small amounts of coffee.

In retrospect, even though they did not fully understand our intentions, they nevertheless allowed us to get their coffee. I remember the first meeting we went into, one of the coffee estate owners, who was much older, said, 'Look I don't want to dissuade you, I'll sell you our coffee, but I think you guys are going to fail.' And I remember thinking, *Oh my God, he doesn't understand what we're trying to do.*

I was unaware that we would need to go convince farms as to what we wanted to do. But then I heard someone from the corner of the room say, 'I understand what they're trying to do.' I looked back and it was his son, who currently runs the coffee plantations.

I came to the realization that, even though we are working to improve the roasting and sourcing processes, the farm itself will undergo significant change as it will now be passed on to the younger generation, who recognize the value of openness and experimentation with premium Arabica.

How did Blue Tokai get its name?

I wanted a name that was distinctly Indian. On one of my farm visits, I remember thinking that it would be amazing to have a name that symbolizes India for us and just then a peacock flew over my head. The peacock is India's national bird. When we searched for names in Indian languages, we discovered that tokai was an ancient Malabari word for peacock. And when we tried to think of a colour to go with it, blue kind of stood out.

Your initial premise was sourcing single-estate Arabica coffee beans from premium Indian coffee estates, roasting them on demand and selling them to leading cafes, restaurants and hotels across the country, as well as selling it online and through B2B partnerships. How did you go about shortlisting coffee estates to source from and how did you convince them to trust you to do business with them, given that you had no background in coffee?

We searched the internet for any company that has received accolades from the Indian Coffee Board or from any other nation. Also, there was a speciality coffee association that listed every coffee company that was a part of the coffee board. We went through that list, called and emailed each one of them, and just kept our fingers crossed that they would reply and most of them did.

It is a small community. What we realized was that the coffee farms knew each other, all of the children had grown up together, they went back so many generations.

So, if we reached out to one person, they would recommend us to somebody else. It was really nice that way. And that was how we made contact. I think we started with four or five estates and have since worked with almost eighty.

What would you say are Blue Tokai's strengths? What has enabled the company to carve out a niche for itself?

I think Blue Tokai's strengths are that it is a full-service company, the number of services and the depth of services that we provide to a customer are unmatched. Also, I think there is a community that really trusts us, and I don't know how we got so lucky with this. For example, we print the estate details, and we have had our customers complain to other brands for not doing the same. We have customers who ask us questions if we haven't made things clear.

It truly means something to me that we have clients who are selectively loyal rather than unconditionally devoted, and I firmly believe that this is one of our strengths. I believe we also place a lot of attention on fostering community growth, whether through coffee events or real cultural events in a manner that I don't see many other businesses doing. For example, there are so many conversations about raising children that are not happening, or are happening behind closed doors.

And since so many conversations happen over coffee, we thought how we can have more of the conversations that happen behind closed doors in public spaces such as cafes. We launched a video series called *Log Kya Kahenge*. The first one is going to be called 'No Filter' and it is going to be about parents raising children or who have started families in different ways. The couple will be the ones communicating with one another. So, Matt and I will discuss our adoption journey.

Additionally, we have a single parent, a co-worker with a neurodivergent kid, and a mother and her transgender daughter who will be discussing their experiences with the condition. Our goal is to build a larger community and facilitate conversations over coffee. I think that has been our speciality and I certainly hope that people find it appealing.

What have been the main challenges of growing a coffee business in a country of tea drinkers? How did social media help you grow your customer base without the benefits of traditional advertising and marketing support?

When we started Blue Tokai we wanted to have a lot of conversations around coffee. Because, as you mentioned, we are a tea-drinking country and we like our drinks really piping hot, sweet and milky, which is also what a lot of people want from coffee.

We provided a range of roast levels to cater to a range of palates. Also, for people who want to experiment with speciality coffee, we have a lot of ready-to-drink and ready-to-brew drinks like Easy Pour and cold brew cans. Easy Pour comes with a premade filter, so you don't need any equipment. And that is really getting popular too.

We have conducted a lot of educational sessions, both offline and on social media and our website, to educate people how to get more out of their coffee, how to determine its quality because we can definitely see a shift in the coffee-drinking culture. Initially we created a lot of pop-ups, social media posts on speciality coffee. We were quite fortunate to have word-of-mouth recommendations. That really helped.

Tell us about the early days of Blue Tokai, when you worked in the spare rooms of your home. Did you ever want to return to the corporate world?

Matt and I would start our work at around 11 in the morning and work until 4 the next morning. We would sift through all the green beans to ensure that there were no stones, no bits that weren't seeds in there. This process would take over two to three hours. And then we would start roasting.

One kilogram would be roasted every hour by our little roaster. And our biggest order in the first two months was a 10-kg order. We still have that photo on our Instagram. So that meant 10 hours of roasting and three hours of sifting beans. While Matt was roasting, I would make all the labels. I would grind all the coffees, stick on the labels, seal all the pouches and pack them up in boxes.

We were working 14- to 16-hour days for about six months before we realized that we were going to have a baby. That was when we hired our first employee, six months into Blue Tokai. Somehow, the roaster decided that every night at 10:30 it was going to conk out and I recall Matt would be on the floor fixing it!

I never ever felt I should go back to the corporate world. Never ever. No matter how stressful it got. I just knew that this was what I wanted to do. I was having fun. I felt an immediate sense of purpose because we were the ones shaping this company. We were literally giving birth to this idea, and the experience was absolutely exciting for me.

What made you decide to take what was essentially a D2C online delivery product into offline cafes? What were the learnings, difficulties and challenges of getting into the café business with absolutely no experience in hospitality?

We had never thought of having an offline cafe. What had happened was that we had found this space in Saidulajab. It was very industrial and very derelict. I remember telling Matt that I feel scared after six o'clock because there are no lights there. So if we have any women coming in here, we will have to escort them down to the main road, for them to get an autorickshaw.

I remember Matt saying, 'We can make this space our own, but if we go to the well-established markets where the vibe was already set we would have no say. I said, 'Fine, let's try it.' And we are so incredibly glad it worked out.

Did you face any obstacles while trying to raise money for your Series A and B? And what do you look for in an investor in terms of shared vision? What has been the funding raised in each round, and what are your expansion plans for the brand?

Regards funding, we were in the process of closing our Series A when COVID hit, so all the offers got pulled back. It was a very difficult time for us but once things stabilized, we were able to put it all together but the whole thing was rather stressful. For Series B, we look for investors with a shared vision. Not all investors want us to be omnichannel, which is definitely the direction we are heading.

Additionally, we are building a sustainable long-term business, which I don't think aligns with hypergrowth and that is something most investors want. I believe that someone who understands our vision— and it is a plus if they know about specialty coffee—is something we truly value in an investor.

What made you decide to go in for a third co-founder and how did Shivam come on board?

Shivam joined us to work in operations and we realized quite soon that he was extremely qualified in areas that we weren't and that the three of us together worked exceptionally well. Shivam played such a massive role in expanding our company that we could see how much he cared for the brand and how valuable he was to us and that was when we decided to make him a co-founder.

What are the advantages and disadvantages of partnering with your spouse?

It goes both ways, it has its advantages for sure because you have this wonderful shared experience and this effort together. The disadvantage is that you don't know when to switch off, so a lot of things from work will spill over into your personal life. Switching off is easier said than done.

Maybe one of you won't, and you will be talking about work. You think you might be able to strike a balance and adhere to work hours and that is great, but I think it is a little bit harder to do. But I do feel very blessed that we both got to do this together. I think it is also our personalities; we are good at different things so we complement each other, whether it is at home or work. I think having a compatible personality is critical.

But I don't think spouses should work together. Because it is a lot of work—you have to work at your relationship as a family, you also have to work at your relationship at work. Also, you both have to be incredibly flexible to hear each other out, grow together and take criticism. It is quite difficult because you are under so much stress to succeed.

I advise you to consider how your partnership will be divided between work and any obligations you have outside of work, such as taking care of your parents or any family member because one person cannot be expected to do both of these things while the other is allowed to do just one. More communication about all of this would be crucial.

For example, how can you expressly and openly say, 'Hey, can you do this week's outside obligation and I can do it next week?'

That would be my advice and that has been my experience as well. I don't think Matt and I had this conversation earlier on, we had to sort of figure it out as we went along and I don't think that was the easiest way to do it. We started this whole thing together but a lot of my responsibility has also been to take care of the kids, while he had a lot of other responsibilities at work. You can't foresee the kind of challenges that could come so I would urge you to think about these earlier on than later.

What does a regular day in your life look like?
I work from home, and a regular day in my life starts with getting my daughters ready for school and dropping the youngest one off to school. Then I come back and look at what I need to do for the day, and get started on meetings. On exceptionally good days, I can get in an hour of exercise in the morning. In the afternoons when my children return from school, I make sure to spend some time going over their homework and then it is back to calls and work. In the evenings when my husband returns from the office, we catch up on how our day went, and after dinner we get the girls ready for bedtime.

And finally, what would you tell women looking to become entrepreneurs?
One of the biggest things I have heard from women who are embarking on or considering embarking on this journey is a complete lack of confidence in themselves even if they are ten times more competent than their male counterparts. They will second-guess themselves while I

see a lot of males who might not even know half as much as the women do, but they will just go and do it. They have just been raised with the confidence to go and do it.

So, one of my tips would be that women must be aware of the imposter syndrome and be confident about their abilities. I think that is a huge deterrent to doing your job well or launching a business. Even in my experience, I have men ignore me and speak directly to my partners, and this is when I helped found this company from scratch. Prepare yourself for that and do not let it control any aspects of your work.

8

"I think a happy mindset is most important because that really helps"

Neelu Khatri

Co-Founder and Senior Vice President International Operations,
Akasa Air

Neelu Khatri burst into the restaurant we were meeting. She was a petite bundle of unbridled energy, the restlessness within her was evident, and yet, she was focused and razor sharp in her responses. She was dressed in comfortable yet chic linen trousers and a top, and knew her mind when she placed the order because there was absolutely no indecision or time wasted trying to choose between options on the menu.

Beneath the easy-going exterior, Neelu Khatri, co-founder and senior vice president-International Operations, Akasa Air, is a tough, no-nonsense woman who knows how to get the work done and how. Being a member of the founding team and establishing an airline from the ground up—from concept to operations—in a single year was no small feat, but she and the founders of Akasa Air have succeeded in doing just that.

It has been a long journey for the young girl from a middle-class home in Jabalpur, a small cantonment town. She was no ordinary girl though. In order to get away from her parents' expectations that she get married after graduating, she chose to take the Air Force entrance exam. She got through making history as one of the first women logistics officers to be recruited into the Indian Air Force (IAF).

And so, on 18 December 1993, she was commissioned into the Indian Air Force. She would spend 15 years in the IAF and had to take premature retirement on 17 December 2008 as wing commander because women were not granted Permanent Commission in the IAF back then.

Life would change again for her. She had to navigate the corporate world, which was completely alien to her. Undaunted, Neelu continued her learning journey, getting an MBA in supply chain management from the Management Development Institute, Gurgaon. She started her corporate career with KPMG, working with Indian and global clients in defence, aerospace and homeland security. She then moved to Honeywell in 2014.

Three years later, she was appointed India president for Honeywell's aerospace business division. She did all this admirably while raising two sons, both of whom were very young when she had to don the mantle of a single mom. Although it was tough, she looks back on those difficulties nonchalantly. Neelu says in a matter-of-fact way, "We made the best of the situation, we had as much fun as we could. We were a happy and adventurous bunch, travelling the country on a brand-new Toyota Innova and discovering many remote Indian cities."

Due to her sheer grit and hard work, she is now the co-founder of Akasa Air, a new entrant in the Indian civil aviation space. She had known Vinay Dube (founder and CEO of Akasa Air) of Jet Airways whom she was in touch with during her time at Honeywell.

After Jet Airways shut down, Vinay was looking at setting up a new airline in India. He came from an international airline background, having returned to India for personal reasons. He was convinced that he could create a world-class airline in India, if he had the right team with him and the right investors. He knew first-hand of Neelu's vast experience in the aviation industry, having interacted with her while she was at Honeywell and picked her to join him.

Launching an airline in India is no mean task; the industry has seen more spectacular collapses and failures than success stories. Entering into this space could be considered an act of utmost bravery. But the team at Akasa Air, including well-regarded airline industry veterans like Vinay Dube and Praveen Iyer, saw the late Rakesh Jhunjhunwala making an initial investment of $ 35 million for a 40 per cent stake, later increasing it to his family now holding around 46 per cent in the airline. Rakesh brought in Aditya Ghosh as a board advisor.

The regulatory and financial procedures itself could daunt lesser souls. Nonetheless, the airline launched on 7 August 2022 with new Boeing 737 MAX 8s. It is arguably the first airline in aviation history to go from zero to twenty aircraft in just 18 months, and it has since grown its fleet to 30 aircraft and more than 1000 weekly flights. By 2027, the airline intends to have 76 aircraft in its fleet. There are also plans to include neighbouring countries to its list of supported locations.

The airline has set itself a target to maintain a ratio of 50 per cent women in each department, and Neelu is enthusiastic about achieving this. When it comes to treating its female employees, even in something as trivial as the cabin crew uniform, the airline is at the forefront. To ensure that they are comfortable while in service, the female cabin crew members don lightweight sneakers made of recyclable materials. Not just the sneakers, the uniform of the crew too is created from recyclable material. And Neelu is determined to ensure that they not only get the gender equality ratio right across departments, but also ensure that Akasa Air is a great place for women to work.

Excerpts from an interview conducted in Mumbai, back in August 2023:

Tell us a bit about your childhood—your family, your parents and early influences. Growing up in Jabalpur 'a sleepy cantt area' as you call it, what were your early dreams for your career?

We came from what I would describe as a lower middle-class family. There was never any dearth of things but at the same time we never forgot how our parents were working to give us the education and the lifestyle we had enjoyed. It was an exceedingly happy childhood; our parents and everybody were so busy making ends meet that the kids in those days were pretty much left on their own. My parents' standing instructions were *'Bas ghar aa jaana sham ko, light shuru honey se pehle. Bulb jalney se pehley ghar ke andar dikhney chahiye'* otherwise we would get a whooping.

The good part is that I had this small Anglo-Indian family in the neighbourhood, and spending time with them made a very big impression on me. We would go to their house as the gentleman (we called him Richard Sir) would give tuitions to kids. Richard Sir was a person with reduced mobility and yet his passionate imagination on the definition of success is what laid a foundation in my mind. Till date, I challenge myself on those very principles of limitless power within.

Since I was Richard Sir's favourite, and we couldn't afford tuitions he would tutor me pro bono. It was there that I developed my English-language skills, which was crucial for a young girl growing up in a small town. It was the first boost that I got because I was better spoken in English than the others in the region, and I could go out in the world with a fair amount of confidence. And I remember when I went for admission to Christchurch in Jabalpur, a convent school, he presented me to the principal who then agreed to give me admission which would have been an impossible task for my parents to get done on their own.

In those days, it was that kind of an environment. I wouldn't characterize myself as a particularly intelligent student, but I was a sincere and diligent one, and I knew I had to concentrate on my studies.

Back then we had the eighth board; before the ten plus two came in, we had the fifth, eighth and eleventh. At the eighth standard you were supposed to choose which subject you would take. This was back in 1984 or '85. What it meant was that I had to choose my subjects in class eight when I did not even understand the importance of studies.

The doors to education in terms of my subject choice closed because I couldn't be interested in math or science to be an engineer; I couldn't be into bio sciences to become a doctor so the only other subject after that was home science. These were the only three choices. And I was miserable studying home science. So, ninth, tenth, eleventh, I studied English, geography, history and cooking and I knew I was a misfit there as well. But whatever was at hand, the importance of sincerity and hard work came in at this time.

I was doing fairly well in those classes, and when I realized that I had to pick some good subjects for college, I decided to take history, economics and other disciplines. The cantonment area around Jabalpur, which was a beautiful town with hills around, was a safe area for a young girl to cycle around, bike around, and it has been my biggest influence. It let me explore the city to my heart's content without my parents worrying about my safety.

How did you end up with the Indian Air Force? Did you face any resistance from your family?

I remember my cousins who were in the *fauj* would always say, *'Neelu, yaar tu fauj ke liye fit hai'*, because I would go around hiking, cycling, biking around Jabalpur. Although people around me could see that I would fit into this environment, women were not allowed in the forces at that time. Therefore, when I finished my college and an advertisement came in the newspapers inviting women to join the IAF, I knew immediately that this was something I wanted to do. I saw this opportunity as a brand-new path that would broaden my life's horizon outside this little city and give me the independence that I craved.

This was in 1992, and the very first reaction from my parents was a resounding no because they could never imagine their daughter would want to go outside Jabalpur and do something. Moreover, the stereotypical image of a *fauji* was that of a strapping, six-footer with a handlebar moustache, so they could never think a woman could be in the fauj. So, the first reaction was understandable. Then they said, 'We are going to get you married off.' My logic was simple—let me go attempt this exam this one time, and if I failed I promised to follow their wishes, even get married.

To be honest, I had absolutely no confidence at the time that I could do anything like this. My exam centre was in Varanasi. And the aptitude test was a written exam. It was heavily skewed towards statistics and maths which I had never studied. So, I was pretty confident that I was going to flunk. But in front of my family, I had to be confident and determined. I picked up several editions of the *Reader's Digest,* bank exam books, monthly and weekly magazines, and I began giving those mock tests, etc., in preparation for the exam.

I found an ex-army colonel who coached aspirants. He charged 500 rupees for three months back then. And I remember breaking my piggy bank and offering the coins tied in a handkerchief to him. He laughed at me and said, 'No, no no, you take this back, I'll still teach you.' I don't know where that gentleman is now, and I regret never going back to meet him because he changed my life. The few classes he gave me made a huge impact. Now when I look back in my life I realize that I am so grateful to these amazing people who stepped into my life miraculously to provide crucial support.

Interestingly, a pleasant incident occurred when I reached Varanasi. There were almost 18,000 or 19,000 applicants from which they chose 18 women candidates from all over India. And mostly, these were women from Delhi, Mumbai, who knew about things, had the confidence. I was from a small town, half their height, sheepish, couldn't speak much and was extremely underconfident. I was extremely nervous because I knew it was a do-or-die situation for me; if I didn't qualify, my life would have been all about staying back in Jabalpur, getting married to a stranger, putting on a *ghunghat,* sitting behind my husband on a scooter and a couple of our kids. That would be my life. It scared me. The pressure was too much. And I think that did the magic!

I still remember my heart racing, as I was sitting on the banks of the river at Varanasi thinking about all this and how it was so important for me to clear the exam. There was this British woman there, who asked me what I was doing alone there on the ghats. When I told her about the exam, she asked me why I was looking so tense.

I confided in her. She listened to me, and then calmly said, 'Neelu, you will make it tomorrow.' She just said it with a finality.

'The first exam you will make it', she told me, 'but you need to worry about the second and the third.'

But I was not worried about those because I knew that those were things that I could do, as they were things that were closer to my DNA. I could debate, actively participate in individual and group activities and ace psychological tests. But maths was what I needed to crack. I took the entrance examinations the following morning, and I was among the select few who passed.

That evening I ran back to the ghats to inform the lady because we had promised each other that I would come back and tell her whatever happened. After I informed her, we started chatting and it was then that she told me she had come to Varanasi to spend her final days because she was dying.

That experience had a huge influence on me, getting that kind of guidance and blessing from someone who was so spiritual, so strong, maybe it was her blessing that motivated me. I was number one in that group. But then of course, it took some time to do the medical, etc.

By the time I reached home, my parents were at a loss of words. They couldn't refuse any more because it was too big an achievement. I was in the first batch of women. There was a lot of talk about it in our family, neighbourhood and social circle. People were dropping in at home, and saying, *'Oh aapki ladki ka ho gaya'*, and I remember Mom wearing that red lipstick of hers and saying, *'Haan ho gaya.'* Suddenly, they became very proud of me, all that *nahin bhejenge*, etc., melted instantly.

Dad had a small dairy in Jabalpur, which sold homemade cheese. My parents were educated to the extent that they could go through in society, but the first thing that strikes me in retrospect is that they neither encouraged nor discouraged me. I was more or less allowed to do as I pleased. I could go make friends, even with boys, and move around freely, which was not allowed by most families. My brother had a Yamaha 100cc and I had a two-wheeler too. So, there were no restrictions that way.

In 1993, you were part of the first batch of women logistic officer in the IAF. What were the challenges of being the first women in this very male space? How did women coming into the forces change things, or the way of doing things?

It was different, and actually it was quite funny and an absolutely fantastic experience. The infrastructure was not in place to handle women. Perhaps the government took the decision because of pressure from many societal segments that women should be brought in, but I don't believe anyone was prepared at the time. The first reaction which most people had was that *ladkiyoon ne aakar isko college bana diya. [Neelu laughs out aloud.]*

With the exception of women in the medical field, who have long been present and are highly respected, the fauj is a couple of centuries old and has always been a male-dominated institution. And they have proven their mettle by enduring extremely tough lives during times of conflict across zones and geographies. I don't think people were unaware of the significance of having women in other branches of the armed forces.

In the corporate space, every little decision we take entails a lot of brainstorming and thinking before it is incorporated. I don't think any of that was done back then. When we reached the Air Force Academy in Dindigul, Hyderabad, for one year of training, the one thing we often heard was, 'Oh, they've spoilt the environment', because now there are boys after girls, girls after boys, and fights between boyfriends and girlfriends. Boys were visiting the women's quarters and vice versa, they were coupling up and all that discipline issues started happening.

The trainers were not trained to handle us. I remember a very amusing incident. Not only did I figure it out early on, but so did every other girl. You know we were woken up for drills at four in the morning. Who likes to do that? The initial reaction was *nahin jaana*, so what excuse would you give? We cited stomach ache, implying that we had our periods and this would make the guys blush. And then they would say, 'Okay go back to sleep.' But wised up soon.

What lessons did your time in the Indian Air Force teach you?
Overall, the atmosphere was quite supportive and instructive. For example, every time we went for that 40-kilometre cross country or the night halts, we always thought how would we be able to do 40 kilometres, that too with the backpacks, the helmet, the rifle. We think we can't but then we realize that no, the mind is much stronger than your body.

It is how you get your body attuned. This, in my opinion, was the most important lesson I learned throughout that one year. In that one year, we underwent strength training, we lost a couple of our course mates and we saw emotional breakdowns. Indian defence officers receive the best training available anywhere in the world. I was a different person after that one year of training.

I spent 16 years in the fauj including that one year of training. You can't go beyond 15 years. Some of my course mates even went to court, but I could not pursue it legally. They won the case, were reinstated and even got adequate compensations. Honestly, my boys were very young when I left the air force. I was aggressively looking out for a job, as I had to bring up my kids, and I could have done either this or that.

The major reason I did not pursue this legally was because I felt I needed to conserve my energy towards something positive.

After 15 years in the supply chain department, you departed from the Indian Air Force in 2008 as an Air Force wing commander. How easy or difficult was it transitioning to the corporate world? Did you have to unlearn or relearn certain things?

I started my corporate career with KPMG, and that was a completely new world. I had to unlearn a lot of stuff and learn a lot of things. Also, with the limited experience, coming into the corporate world was a task. It was challenging and a bit degrading as well especially if I thought of myself as a senior officer. I was equated with fresh college graduates (even worse—I did not even know how to operate a laptop!).

I joined as an assistant manager, or as I like to call myself, a government relations person, assisting the teams in understanding government bids and whom to speak with. As a former government officer, I would always know how and whom to carve a path within those corridors effectively. But after two to three months, I realized that I don't want to be a glorified door opener. I really wanted to make something out of my life, which is when I spoke to my mentor within the company and the then deputy CEO of KPMG Richard Rekhy. I shared my angst and dissatisfaction regarding my current role with him. It was Richard who challenged me to think out of the box and create what I was good at an 'aerospace and defence' advisory practice.

Now, when I share my experiences with other young ladies, I advise them to find their mentors. If you do this, you'll discover people who can relate to and support you, just like I did at KPMG. I walked up to Richard and shared that I wanted to leave because this is the situation I am facing. He said, 'Don't worry, we know you have a good DNA of work, so let me know what you want to do.' I said that I wanted to be in a management consulting job and requested him to give me a chance. And I was offered an opportunity. Till date I wonder why Richard even gave me this opportunity—I had no corporate presence, no management consulting experience—but sometimes your mentors see in you what you don't.

This is how we ended up creating an aerospace, aviation and defence advisory, and we were the first of the Big Four to open it. This was in 2008 and during that time, we were working with the Airport Authority of India handing over the airports to GMR as a privatization process. I was familiar with these kinds of initiatives. With larger organizations like KPMG, I got some fantastic exposure to its global offices.

I have always had the mindset that I can't do this work. I never thought, *I know a lot.* I knew that whatever I knew was irrelevant here. I would have only deceived myself if I attempted to project my confidence or overconfidence. I therefore had no qualms about approaching the junior-most person, sitting with them and taking in their knowledge if I could see that I could learn from them. I did this for the first year-and-a-half. One thing that became clear to me, in both in my defence forces life and now in the corporate world, that the foundational importance of good leadership and teamwork cannot ever be overestimated and my learnings from the air force came in handy here.

Project management skills was another that came in handy. You needed to work to a plan, adhere to deadlines, have clarity on 'to-do list', all of which are necessary in any field. I started doing that and thinking more clearly, delivering my message more effectively, and collaborating with the IIM and IIT alumni. I remember my first jump was from assistant manager to director, from a package of Rs 9 or 10 lakh to Rs 40 lakh or something like that. Again, my mentor Richard Rekhy (by then the CEO at KPMG) pushed me to believe in myself.

I don't think people had even heard of a jump like that and there were people who were betting on me, saying let's see how long she lasts. Some of those colleagues are my best friends now, and they told me at my farewell, 'Oh Neelu, we're so proud that you made it this far in KPMG.' So, it was tough but I really don't think there was anything melodramatic about it, or negative about it. Be happy and go with the flow and take each day at a time have always been my mantras of life.

So, while I had done a short MBA course from IIM Ahmedabad and another one from MDI Gurgaon, I seized any chance the company provided for internal trainings. I never went with an attitude that I know what leadership is because of my experience in the forces; corporate leadership is very different. I have always leaped at whatever courses they could offer, one-day, two-day meet up with as many people as I could.

If there was a team coming in from another country, I would make sure senior leaders would give me 10 or 15 minutes of their time and I would go sit with them and ask them if they could tell me how to go about things. I always made a lot of effort to reach out to people and get their thoughts. This way I would get plenty of new business ideas and tips on how to implement.

By 2013, I had done a lot of consulting at KPMG but I always felt a gap in my experience on the operations. When the Honeywell opportunity came, I eagerly took it up because it was such a good brand. It was here that I learnt about the ins and outs of profit and loss statements, how to do business, how to do sales, how to work with engineers to develop products. And understand the client's perspective. Honeywell is a gold standard company when it comes to operational processes and quality and my learnings in these next five years was absolutely chiselled. It was an extremely rich experience for me with a steep learning curve. It was a pan-global experience because I was working with the team in Europe, which was the headquarters, as well as the manufacturing and the service centres in the US and China respectively.

By this time, I had groomed myself into a corporate person, which was a powerful experience. As a part of Honeywell, I was interacting with Vinay Dube, the then CEO of Jet Airways and now the founder of Akasa. He came from Delta Airlines and returned to India because he wanted to be with his parents in their last years. He is extremely sharp, mathematical and a global citizen with extensive experience in the airlines industry. I was at Honeywell and he was at Jet. I would go to sell my APUs and avionics, so we kept in touch. And then, Jet Airways died and could not be revived. One thing I also realized at this time is that building relationships and networking with individuals are crucial. Women don't do it as well as men. I think I had a knack for it. I would keep in touch with my ex-colleagues, I would find time to sit with people and just chat. I keep telling women around me to invest in networking with people. They are the ones who will actually provide you advice or support when you need it.

After I left Honeywell, I was running a small consulting firm of my own, and then COVID happened, and Vinay and I touched base. He was out of Jet Airways. Vinay told me he was thinking of launching an airline. There were already three or four people with him. I asked him if there was anything I could do to help. And he said, 'I need help with the government, regulatory approvals, I don't know that part. And if that doesn't go well with me, I'm not going to launch an airline.' And I told him, 'Vinay, don't worry about that because I will take care of it.' And I added, 'I will also do it with absolutely no under-the-table dealing because I know how to work with the Indian government.'

While a lot of people say a lot of things about the Indian bureaucracy, I knew right from my KPMG days that you can collaborate with people anyway you wanted. You see, corruption is never one way, it is always a two-way mechanism. We can't just blame the person taking the bribe, the person giving it is equally to be blamed. I was confident that I could handle this part very well, so I started working with the team. While Vinay and the others were busy with raising money, and talking to the aircraft and the engine makers, I spent the first year-and-a-half in getting the regulatory permissions in place because without that we couldn't launch the airline. Then one fine day, the government gave us the licence to run it, and we were like, 'Hey, what do we do now?' We put everything in place on 7 August 2022 and began operations.

The core team consisted of highly experienced people who had previously worked with Jet and Go Air. Since Vinay came with a global experience, Airbus and Boeing believed in him. And he was surrounded by a team comprising the best from commercial, IT, finance, leasing, etc.

The one lesson that emerges from all this is that you need to surround yourself with people who are better than you. When you form a team like that you are bound to succeed. You can't act as though I am going to hire people who will follow my orders. Each one of us was doing our thing; nobody was interfering. For instance, if I was handling the government affairs, I was just running it on my own because I knew the goals I had created.

In a similar vein, there were other people independently working on the commercial side, leasing side, contractual side, etc. So, as a group we worked cohesively, with a lot of transparency, nobody was sitting on anyone's head or breathing down their neck.

RJ [*Rakesh Jhunjhunwala*] was thrilled to meet us and invest in Akasa. He believed that this was an investment for his kids. Obviously, he wasn't doing well physically and he knew that. The faith he showed in us and the vision that he had about India greatly influenced us.

Since he had a strong belief in the Indian economy and felt that the country would grow enormously, it was obvious to him that an airline would succeed. At the time, 150 million tickets were sold annually, so he reasoned that if everyone began to travel you are looking at growing three to four time at the minimum. He simply assumed that professionals were doing the job well.

A year-and-a-half before we started, the six of us who got together began creating the plan. Once we met Rakesh Jhunjhunwala and he invested in it, we became the core group of founders. I don't think anyone of us works like a founder or a co-founder. For example, I oversee international operations and somebody looks after finance. It is more about all of us, there are nine of us, of which three are women. It is a highly professionally run organization, where a lot of debate and a lot of thinking are encouraged. We don't want to encourage a promoter-driven corporate mindset like many other airlines, which we don't relate to.

You are committed to having 50 per cent women in the workforce at Akasa. How is that coming along?

Although having 50 per cent female employees is undoubtedly a difficult goal, it may be relatively simple for an airline to achieve this because there are many female crew members. Therefore, the first decision made by the Akasa leadership was to have both men and women on the crew, rather than just women. The second was that diversity numbers in various divisions must be considered when examining diversity. You can't say that in engineering you have only 2 per cent and in crew you have 50 per cent or 70 per cent. It needs to be measured department by department.

You have said in one of your early interviews, 'Even if I was sitting at home, I would have created something.' What are the alternative careers that you might have explored if the Indian Air Force had not come into your career path?

I am not the type of person who would have been satisfied with doing nothing. I would have taken up a social cause. I come from Madhya Pradesh, a land rich in tribal art and artefacts. I am sure I would have picked up something or the other.

Raising two boys as a single parent, working in a demanding job at first at the Indian Air Force, then at KPMG and Honeywell, that must have been extremely challenging. How did you juggle your responsibilities as a parent and a senior corporate executive?

First of all, it is important to cultivate a positive outlook. That has always been my approach to life. When I look back, my kids also felt the same. The three of us were a happy bunch, jumping around to eat at McDonald's and going to watch *Spiderman* movies. I drew a lot of my enthusiasm from my kids, I made sure they got what they desired, for instance, football training. We would be completely broke but we would figure out how to eat dinner in a five-star hotel. We would finish our dinner at home and then go to Maurya Sheraton and order a bowl of soup with breadsticks, and ask for one more basket of bread. For that one soup, I clearly recall paying Rs 300 to sit comfortably and enjoy myself. I think a happy mindset is the most important because that really helps.

I think kids of single moms are incredibly empathetic. My boys value whatever I could give them in whatever form. I recall how hard it was for me to even buy them a pair of football shoes, so nothing was ever taken for granted. When my son was in college in the US it was minus 20–30 degrees there sometimes, but he was grateful that he had the opportunity to study there, so he ensured that he was thrifty.

He would be walking around with a hole in his shoe; that one time I literally had to show him my bank account and tell him that we had enough money to afford a new pair of shoes.

Now he works for Microsoft. He is 29. The other one is five years younger, and both of them have good memories of our time at fauj where their personalities were shaped.

How does Neelu Khatri unwind after a hectic workday? I read somewhere that you would like to become a bus driver, how did that retirement plan come about?

If I'm in the kitchen, I love to cook. I enjoy baking a lot. I bake different types of cakes. I read a lot and watch a lot of movies. I like travelling and hiking. I take great pleasure in motorbiking, though I had lost touch with it and am picking it up slowly. I am a serious hiker. I have completed the Annapurna trek in Nepal, and I will pick it up more and more as I go forward. I intend to continue being physically active for the next 15 to 20 years. I have realized that we are the ones who set the physical boundaries of our abilities.

I recall, once we had to cross a freshly cut corn field full of stubs while on a hike. We walked with high steps to avoid getting get hurt. We continued to plod despite our exhaustion when our instructor sergeant abruptly halted and yelled at us. We were still going at a strong pace even though the corn field was a kilometre behind us! We conditioned our bodies to react a certain way to our surroundings because our bodies stopped experiencing pain and we were walking in a robotic manner. What we need to do is be aware of this and not let this limit us.

I had a brief tour of a few museums while travelling through the United States aboard a bus. I felt exhausted after visiting four or five museums; you see, I am not a big fan of museums, so I rested in the bus and struck up a conversation with the driver. It turned out that he was a CEO of an IT software company and had resigned a couple of years ago. He was just doing this to keep himself busy. I too want to feel and do nothing that demands mental energy.

I really want to go and work in an Amazon factory just boxing parcels, or be a bus driver where a lot of physical hard work is required. I am certain that I am going to do something like that for a few years of my life. Or be a waitress somewhere. People don't realize how nice it feels to just unwind. I want to experience all kinds of labour-intensive work. [*Neelu smiles with a twinkle in her eyes.*]

If there is one message you would like to share with women and girls reading this, what would it be?

Women are a hardworking lot in their DNA. We are designed differently. It is not natural to us to promote ourselves as effortlessly as men do. We lose track easily especially when we are thrown a choice between career and family or kids or husband. We crumble under pressure. The fact remains that women are much stronger than men, they can multitask, they can give birth to kids and even raise them singlehandedly, so obviously they can tolerate more pain. However, for thousands of years, women have been conditioned to believe that they are incapable of doing certain things—you can't be angry, you can't be aggressive. Whether we like it or not, all of us are affected by this social conditioning.

This will not go away until we are conscious of the limitations we set for ourselves. It is important for us to recognize what our boundaries are, and understand who has set these for us and why, and how can we expand these limitations just a little bit—we will all do wonders if we think that way.

Once, my neighbour requested me to talk to her daughter out of becoming a surgeon because it would be difficult to find a more qualified groom than her. I was aghast. Although our thinking is superior to that of the West, a lot of it is still very backward. We often confine ourselves within boundaries set for us by others. We need to be conscious of the subconscious boundaries set by ourselves, our families or our society, and break free.

I feel exceptionally happy and fortunate about the opportunity that I have got in my life to witness the changing world and move with it. I get inspired by the younger lot of women entrepreneurs who work with a force and no inhibitions. Be fearless—what is the worst that can happen—has been a motto of my life.

What's a typical day in your life like?
My typical day includes some form of high intensity workout or a simple run on the treadmill, healthy diet, and routine office work and meetings. On weekends, I make it a point to plan short hikes outside of Mumbai city or just going to a good restaurant.

9

"But when you start internalizing the problems, you become part of the problem"

Rachana Gupta
Co-Founder,
Gynoveda

How did the need for a sabbatical from the corporate world, one woman's quest for happiness, a search for a permanent cure for the psoriasis that had been plaguing her husband all come together to create the world's first femtech (female technology) company that combined technology and ayurveda to help women address and resolve their gynaecological problems?

It seems like an unlikely story, given that Rachana Gupta, then in her mid-forties and on a sabbatical from the BPO industry where she had been in leadership roles for almost two decades, had absolutely no background either in ayurveda or entrepreneurship, but strangely enough, all these—the sabbatical, the quest for happiness and the search for permanent relief from psoriasis—served as the catalysts to put into motion an enterprise that would now become Gynoveda. She had been searching for purpose, and with Gynoveda, a business idea that came almost serendipitously to her, she found it.

Rachana calls herself an accidental entrepreneur. Coming from a traditional middle-class, Konkani family, the rough and tumble of entrepreneurship was not something she was familiar with because she had always seen her father and the other men in the neighbourhood go off to office in the morning and return in the evening.

But entrepreneurship was going to be part of her destiny, even if she did not know it back then as a young girl growing up in the western Mumbai suburb of Goregaon, and attending St Thomas High School, where she and her to-be husband, Vishal, were classmates from kindergarten.

They started dating in college, and eventually got married. They were both in the corporate space, they had a young son, Soham, life was complete. But there was a niggling feeling in Rachana's mind that there should be more to life, and it compelled her to take a sabbatical and go on a quest for happiness. She trained to become a happiness coach, and even wrote a book about it, titled *Happiness ki Khoj*.

At the same time, Vishal too set off on a quest to find a cure for the psoriasis that had been plaguing him for years. Little did both of them imagine this would eventually lead them to discover the power of ayurveda, which eventually would have both of them step away from the corporate world to set up Gynoveda, in partnership with Dr Arati Patil, an ob-gyn and an ayurveda practitioner.

Gynoveda is the world's first femtech company combining ayurveda and technology. It serves more than five lakh women a month, and saw its customer base increase a thousand times during the pandemic when women could not visit their gynaecologists. They created the world's very first Period Bot that allowed women to self-diagnose their period problems on their mobile through a short quiz, which was powered by an AI backend, after which they could have a WhatsApp consultation with an expert for medication and treatment options.

This allowed women to avoid visiting a clinic for consultation when struggling with gynaecological disorders like PCOD, PCOS, endometriosis, fibroid, cysts. At the time of writing this, women across 180 countries had taken the test on the Gynoveda Period Bot, providing the company with a wealth of information about women's menstrual health globally.

In 2019, Gynoveda received their seed funding of $1 million from Fireside Ventures. Their Series A funding led by India Alternatives Fund raised $10 million in 2023. The round also saw participation from reputed family offices and institutions including Wipro Enterprises, RPG Ventures, Dharampal Satyapal Ltd and Alteria Capital.

Fireside Ventures also participated in the Series A funding round. The money was used for R&D to develop new ayurvedic products, to expand the team and distribution channels as well as increase brand awareness. To this end, the brand signed on actor Taapsee Pannu to be their brand ambassador. The brand has recently switched from online-first model to an offline play of India's first chain of ayurveda fertility clinics.

With Gynoveda, Rachana has found her purpose, her *ikigai* as she says. And with her endeavour, she has not only brought ayurveda out of the shadows by integrating it with technology via an app, but also created a safe space for women to reach out to for information, support and help that they might not otherwise have access to.

Excerpts from an interview conducted in Mumbai in September 2023:

I know you grew up in Goregaon, Mumbai, and attended St Thomas High School, where you and your spouse were classmates. What was your childhood like? What was your family like?

I have an elder sister and a brother. I was raised in a traditional Konkani Goud Saraswat Brahmin home, with my dad working and my mother staying at home. I call her my happiness maker. My father worked in Larsen & Toubro for 32 years. He rose through the ranks. He had a traumatic childhood. Of course, I realized the impact of it only much later.

For him to have left his hometown, which is this quaint little village called Ankola, nestled on the border between Goa and Karnataka, at the age of 17 without any parental support, and coming to Mumbai and starting his career in the Railways and then moving to Larsen & Toubro, pretty much shaped how the three of us have been brought up. It is all about grit, resilience, sticking to a regime and leading a disciplined life. And doing that without being devoid of happiness.

Because of him being in L&T, we were able to visit some of the most beautiful vacation houses in the nation, including Kodaikanal, Ooty and Darjeeling. We had great family trips, great family time and great family holidays. I don't think I was deprived of anything, but it was all measured. When I reflect on it, I believe that I had a joyful childhood.

The one thing that I completely owe to my parents is that they never held the opinion that their kids could not pursue their dreams. I was raised to think that I will do what will make me happy. In our home, success was about doing what makes you happy.

So, Dad is truly Haanikarak Bapu and absolutely identical to what Aamir Khan's role was in *Dangal*. He was behind his daughters to make sure they become winners. In our home, the pressure was on the son and the daughters were pampered unlike how it is in most Indian homes. I think, we were raised by a feminist dad who made it amply evident that all three children would have equal opportunities.

I became the family's black sheep since Dad was so picky about what his two older children would do. My brother was a trophy child who completed his engineering degree at VJTI and my sister became an architect, both of them completed their master's degrees in the United States. By the time it was my turn, Dad was like 'Okay, I'm done. Choose whatever you want.'

I took complete advantage of that and I chose commerce at Narsee Monjee College of Commerce and Economics. After that, I was certain that I wanted to pursue an MBA. I honestly did not know what an MBA would be but it sounded so fancy, more so when the other kids chose conventional academic paths.

Ironically, despite having an MBA in marketing, I never held a marketing-related position until now, with this entrepreneurial stint. My career choices were pretty much well defined in my head. I completed my MBA from Lala Lajpatrai College in Mumbai. While pursuing my MBA, I discovered that, although I am not sure if I have a knack for marketing, I excelled at building relationships with people rather than closing deals. Thus, it revealed a new aspect of my personality that I was aware of, but I doubt I realized how powerful it was.

Thankfully, I knew what to do about it. I hated my first job with Kimberley-Clark as a sales professional. It was then that I realized I didn't want to be in sales. I got married in the year that I graduated, that is, 2000. Vishal and I had been dating for five years. We came from diverse backgrounds—he being a Baniya and I a Kokanastha

Brahmin. Vishal was not just any Baniya, but the one who hailed from one of those families that loves to eat, loves to talk about food, I think they actually live to eat.

In our Konkani household, food serves a practical purpose, you eat because it is essential for your well-being. I honestly think my love for food began after my marriage into the Gupta parivar. On the professional front, I moved into the BPO industry since it was mushrooming in India at that time. Y2K has been quite instrumental in my life both professionally and personally.

When you were working in sales in Kimberly-Clark, did you ever consider becoming an entrepreneur?

Never. You'll find it difficult to believe that I never thought about it until the age of 44–45. I was clearly an accidental entrepreneur. Vishal is an intentional entrepreneur. It is in his blood, it is in his DNA, that Baniya *jugaad,* the Baniya street smartness, by virtue of his father having exposed him to the business side of things at the age of 21 or 22.

I had a different upbringing and background. Dad would return home by 6:30 in the evening, have his chai and snacks and take our case one after the other, and that was where the whole Haanikaarak Bapu got in, literally *ek ke baad ek, sabka number aata tha.*

He wanted my elder sister to become a doctor so the pressure on her was more, clearly it was Viru Sahastrabuddhe of *3 Idiots*. And my brother had to become an engineer. I think it clearly came from Dad's own insecurities of not having a formal education.

We were a hard-core middle-class working family with no exposure to business. Dad had a job and there were family discussions about the budget, how much was allocated for what and how much we could splurge and so on. No one in my extended family was into business as well. We simply did not have a risk-taking mindset, nor were we encouraged to have one.

For want of a better analogy, let me put it this way: We were not hunters, we were essentially farmers. My in-laws are hunters. They can easily figure out how to make one plus two is equal to four and we are happy with one plus two is equal to three. We struggle all our lives to convert the three into four.

I detested going on the field every day when I was working with Kimberly-Clark. I don't think I am capable of complaining about anything due to my upbringing. So, I couldn't be in a job where I had to complain. Thankfully, the BPO industry was right there, ready to embrace people.

I began my career in the BPO industry in 2001 and I worked in it for 17 years. I had my fair share of sabbaticals, like when I had Soham, or when I needed to take some time out.

It was during one of your sabbaticals that you trained as a happiness coach and wrote your book Happiness ki Khoj. ***How did this come about?***

I was curious about what happiness really means to several people. I truly felt I belonged in the BPO space. I think that somewhere in my journey, I became an advocate of women's well-being. Working with sizable, female-focused teams also helped to foster it, and my former COO at Intelinet Global Services, Radhika Balasubramaniam, was also instrumental in shaping the kind of woman I am today.

On the home front, having a mother who silently defended herself and her kids by standing up for what she believed in, helped. My elder sister quietly became an architect and went on to pursue her dreams, so I think, women building women was fairly prevalent in my life. I did see a lot of sisterhood stories unfolding in my subconscious or sphere of influence.

I think reporting to a woman senior at work helped bring a lot of issues to the fore. I believe it was being inspired by how she rose through the ranks completely on merit. There were many women leaders, it was not like I was the only woman in the boardroom, but we were clearly in a minority. However, how to be unapologetically myself and how to do that without any guilt, came to the forefront.

I think I felt glad to finally just be able to express myself without having to worry about what people think because that did not happen at home. I did not know why should I be anyone else at work. There were conversations happening and we were getting labelled, but I kind of developed a thick skin to all of that.

Sure, we did get affected initially by the prejudices women face, but we learnt how to handle it thanks to my ex-boss who was a complete outlier in a male-dominated industry. She was a fierce woman, and our conversations made me realize that how as women we needed to go out there and demand what we deserve.

These were some of the lessons that went into shaping me into what I would become as a young mother. As a young mother, getting back into the BPO workspace was challenging. I believe that the world is cruel and may bring you down, even if you have a wonderful support network and a husband who is always there for you. The last thing you want is people at work to judge you because you are already dealing with so much criticism at home.

My aunts taunted me for outsourcing the care of my child because I was working in the outsourcing sector. I had all kind of accusations thrown my way.

I was interacting with a lot of young mothers in my workspace. And we were all voicing grievances, and I am not referring to only house helps or receiving the necessary assistance at home. We were unhappy about the glass ceiling. But when you start internalizing the problems, you become part of the problem. I have always believed in finding solutions, I hate complaining. And I saw a lot of that. That was when I realized that in order to offer women perspective, someone needs to just show them that they need to check if their glass is half full or half empty.

The thought stayed there. I was happy doing my job, I loved being a working mother, despite the fact that I missed out on so many of my son's competitions, probably wasn't around for some of his milestones, but in hindsight if I had to go back I would do it again, in exactly the same way. So, I felt that women needed to be shaken a little and given a reality check about what constant complaining would achieve versus seeing the whole picture and trying to find solutions. I decided to take a corporate sanyas. This was in 2016. The period was quite uncertain.

It felt like a kind of a void after having worked for 15 to 16 years. I felt clueless about the future. So, I thought let me get certified to be a happiness coach, and I enrolled myself for the course A Life of Happiness and Fulfilment, taught by Professor Raj Raghunathan, aka Dr Happysmarts, the only happiness professor in the Ivy League colleges. It included more than just the ephemeral discussions; it included the entire science of happiness. I started blogging at the same time as I started doing that.

My very first blog was on a platform called Mompresso. Writing proved cathartic for me. After that, there were numerous encounters with women, and it became clear that they needed to be encouraged to see the positive side of things. So that was the idea of the book, and that was how it got published. I decided earlier on to self-publish. I didn't know if I wanted to be an author, but I definitely knew that I wanted to do something in the space of happiness.

There was no commercial aspect to it; it was purely about expressing my feelings. I now believe that my decision to self-publish it was a result of my naivety. It was more for friends and family, and completely in that space. Of course, I got advice that I should get it traditionally published, but to get into the traditional publishing space I would have to totally rewire myself. I couldn't be operating from where I am.

One very obvious realization that emerged as a result of the book was how women deprioritize their own health and well-being. I had witnessed certain aspects of it even in my BPO days—how women in pain were scared to take leave. Instead, they popped painkillers, as they wanted some quick-fix solutions. And also, there was this whole trivializing of women's issues.

I mean, we ourselves trivialize PMS and keep laughing at it, so how can we expect men to take our gynaecological issues seriously? I saw a lot of confusion in the space, but I wasn't saying that I want to do something about it. So, all this became part of my subconscious, and by virtue of the book, and my interactions with hundreds of women, I have realized that we deprive ourselves by prioritizing the well-being of our families, our kids and everything else.

How did you choose to start your business in this field when you had no prior experience with ayurveda or women's health? Was there a catalyst that led you down the path?

So, while I was busy with my happiness book, a parallel track was going on in Vishal's life. He was diagnosed with psoriasis, and we struggled with it for almost seven to eight years, without finding a cure. And after all those years of suffering and witnessing his father suffer from severe psoriasis, I believe his paranoia began to develop.

He kept saying, 'I'm just in my early 30s, and I don't want to be in the same situation as my father.' He tried everything, from going to quacks, to consulting the best of doctors at the best of hospitals, but to no avail. Vishal had surrendered to the fact that he just needs to control this, not cure this. He was in Delhi when someone from his extended family gave him a CD of Rajiv Dixit.

In India, Rajiv Dixit is counted among the first to spread awareness for ayurveda. Vishal listened to Dixit's CD with an open mind, and tried some concoctions that he prescribed. I was sceptical and reluctant because we had already done so much, and now one more, but he was extremely determined, and said, 'If this doesn't work, nothing after this.'

And so, he started applying various concoctions on the affected areas, drank a lot of amla juice and soaked fennel seeds among many other. He did this for the period recommended, and the psoriasis miraculously vanished completely.

I was obviously relieved that he would no longer have to deal with anxiety and paranoia, but I don't think I was particularly convinced about ayurveda. I found the treatment to be cumbersome and hence very inconvenient—something that we might take up if there was an extreme case. However, we had been so accustomed to our own modern medicine or allopathy for so long that there was not really any reason to consider ayurveda as a possibility. Vishal, on the other hand, was convinced of its efficacy and delved deep to improve his understanding of ayurveda.

A year later, I think in 2017, I contracted dengue. Using an ayurvedic mixture that he did not prepare himself but purchased from a local store, Vishal treated me himself and cured me of dengue in three days. He visited the store after learning about the cure from Baba Ramdev and Rajiv Dixit.

The physician there recommended a syrup, which arrested my rapidly declining platelets. I was back on my feet within three to four days. That incident, in my opinion, convinced me of the effectiveness of ayurveda in a way that I don't believe any other success tale has done.

After that, we started implementing it on Soham. As children do when they are young, Soham used to have colds and cough frequently, especially during the monsoon months when school was back in session.

When we started giving him ayurvedic cough remedies, we were out of medicines in no time. As a family we had then embraced ayurveda in a big way, it got ingrained my DNA. That was when the book came out. While I was still on a sabbatical, Vishal was working. He had then 20 years of experience in the digital space, digital first ecommerce experience, having worked with Cleartrip, ACKO, Reliance Jio. At a particular point, everyone around us began telling us to do something big about ayurveda since we were such great believers of the ancient Indian holistic system of medicine.

People had seen how we had benefited from ayurveda. We started asking ourselves, 'Can we open a clinic?' We had some money to invest after having worked so hard for so many years. So, we searched online and found a young ayurvedic doctor, Dr Manaan Gandhi, son of a famous politician.

Barely 27 or 28 years old, Manaan was practising from his house in Juhu and had a fabulous understanding of ayurveda. He mastered *naadi pariksha* the core of ayurveda. We decided to angel invest in a clinic called The Integral Ayurveda in Santa Cruz. That is where Dr Manaan continues to practise. This was early 2018.

Why did you decide to focus on women's health, and specifically gynaecological health issues? And why did you feel a tech-based app could redress it?

I was spending a lot of time at the clinic, which was visited by many young women with menstrual and reproductive disorders like PCOS, irregular periods, heavy bleeding, fibroids, endometriosis, vaginal infections, and such. At that time, I had no idea that ayurveda has a remedy for these problems.

Historically, ayurveda has always been known to successfully treat lifestyle disorders, diabetes, asthma, respiratory asthma, osteoporosis. I saw that it worked, but it took time. We spoke to the women, to ascertain their main reason behind seeking a cure with ayurveda. Was it their decision or their parents'?

After that, we conducted a lot of secondary research to understand the market and determine the scope of the problem. We were absolutely taken aback with our findings. At that point, we realized that going from one clinic to another clinic might not be the answer. We asked ourselves, 'Why don't we create a digital-first solution?'

That was when Gynoveda was born. This was in late 2020. Gynoveda combines ayurveda, technology, content and community to solve fertility, PCOS, period-related disorders. We didn't start the e-commerce portal right away. And we agreed that procrastination can occasionally ruin a good idea, so we decided to avoid it. We decided to evaluate whether the market was as big enough as we estimated it to be. We felt the need to bring in a specialized doctor in women's reproductive health.

A general practitioner wouldn't work. We soon discovered a wonderful doctor who is our third partner at Gynoveda today, Dr Arati Patil. She is an MD Obstetrics and an ayurvedic gynaecologist. She ran her own practice in Shastri Nagar, Lokhandwala. I still recall going to her clinic and completing the registration form while posing as a client. And when I went in I told her, 'Thankfully I'm in excellent health, but I have a business proposition for you.'

I have asked her many times since, 'Why did you not throw me out of your clinic?' And her answer was that she was tired of just sitting in one clinic, and she was looking for something new to do. She was this rare combination of an ayurveda doctor who went on to do her MD in Switzerland. That was where she got exposed to the issues that menopausal, perimenopausal women experience. So somewhere all the three of us were meant to be partners in our new venture.

Vishal and I are two different sides of the same coin that have come beautifully together. We have never sat each other down and said, 'We are done with the corporate world, let's do something different.'

Many people find it difficult to believe, yet our decision to work together just happened naturally. We did discuss the pros and cons, but not whether we should work together. Whether husband and wife should be starting their own business is a matter for another book.

What kind of research did you do and what gaps did you discover in this space?

Before the term Gynoveda was even coined, we had secondary data but we had to look at the primary data. This led us to build the world's first period test. A woman can answer 20 questions on Gynoveda.com from anywhere in the world. It is an AI-based test with an algorithm running at the backend. Based on your answers, you can determine whether or not you have a particular menstrual disorder, and I believe that really blew up in terms of the type of responses we received.

As of today, more than six lakh women from 180 countries have taken the test. For us, that turned into a treasure trove of information about the particular issues facing Indian women. Health problems like PCOS, irregular periods, infertility seemed to be the biggest problem areas and then COVID struck.

Since the pitching stage can occasionally discourage or intimidate female entrepreneurs, what lessons did you gain from it?

I would always ask the investor if they needed an elevator pitch of four minutes, a 40-minute pitch or a detailed four-hour pitch. And tailor my pitch accordingly. Sometimes you have covered a lot of ground and by the time you get to the meat, the investor has lost interest.

It is like *Shark Tank,* investors are meeting entrepreneurs dime a dozen. An investor's enthusiasm is all that I require to share my back story and accomplishments. Very soon, I realized that it would be ideal if we asked them what they wanted right at the start.

Vishal felt that was really curt, but then I said there was nothing curt about it. If they want a four-minute pitch, I would just show them the numbers. And if they want four hours, we can start right from the time the enterprise was born.

We had no revenue at first, but when we made about Rs 50,000, we made a proposal to Fireside Investors, who are now both our seed investor and our growth partners, as well as our Series A investors. For me, that was the time when I really understood as to what I was going to transition into. From a corporate professional to a happiness coach to suddenly pitching a business idea. And I did not even know how I got here in the first place—I mean, there can't be a greater man's world than the investor world.

I think that was when all my inhibitions just fell because there was no way I could fake it no matter how hard I tried. I am not saying they are vultures or going to judge you, but they can be harsh and tactical. Your ability to answer questions and provide an answer affect whether you are in the game or not. I didn't want to mess it up for Vishal.

He always had an entrepreneurial streak. He was so passionate about doing something of his own and I derived all my energy from him. So, I did not want to ruin it for him because he really deserved it. When I went in, I realized that, boss, I am just learning the tricks of the trade, and it was not that difficult at all. It does not matter if you did not ace maths in school. Somebody else will do the maths for you.

How important is it to find a good fit with your investors? Has there been any instance where you have realized that investor fit might not work? How many investors did you have to approach before Fireside Ventures signed up for the seed funding?

At least fifty. In the first place, they simply couldn't wrap their heads around the fact that we had absolutely no experience or background in this field, and wanted to operate in this space. So, we were tested, burnt, fried, roasted, all of that. [*Rachana laughs out loud.*] I think our partnership with Fireside Ventures is a love story of sorts. It is crucial to find the right match.

An important factor I think is our age, we were older founders with more maturity. Vishal and I were fortunate to be on the same side of the table and were quite clear about what we wanted to accomplish and what we did not want to do. There have never been any serious disagreements. In my opinion, it is simpler to be open and truthful in marriages where the couple first became friends before being married. Sure, there were times when someone was ready to put in the money and Vishal was ready to go with it but I refused and vice versa.

With Fireside, I think it is quite safe to say that when we entered that room, we had at least viewed the entire scene from the perspective of a seed fund. Dr Arati and I were in a room with 10 gentlemen for our three-hour presentation, and it was quite encouraging to hear how comfortable I felt discussing how menstrual health can improve women's lives. It was heartening to see that nobody squirmed in their chairs, and they were staring at me directly.

There was this lovely vibe about building this together and co-creating, so somewhere there were synergies. They were interested in health tech and women's health; it was part of their investment thesis, but I think they were also seeking founders who were mature enough to say that they would seek advice rather than attempt to create it themselves if they were unsure. Somewhere there was a lot of personality match and shared vision; it all came together and that was how our partnership began.

The transition from service to product is undoubtedly challenging. Given that ayurvedic products are a complicated marketplace and there is an issue with trust, what were the challenges you faced in setting it up?

Because we went digital first, it was important for us to work on the trust markers and build credibility. We were clear that we were not a product company, we were a content-and education-led company. We were not there to sell products, we were there to educate women about their problems, what will happen and how ayurveda will help them.

Thus, the whole machinery of content to commerce began with that mindset. It was never about how many units we are selling daily. We were confident that we were creating a legacy brand that would transcend the three of us and eventually surpass our combined contributions. By then, Vishal and I had interacted with over 200 doctors and 2,000-odd consumers, so we said can we break the scepticism about ayurveda as a solution to gynaecological issues by building evidence that it works. We focused on evidence-based science and not conviction-based science alone.

All our product formulations have all the necessary certifications, including FDA India approval, FSSAI or GNP certification. We were clear that we were not going to cut corners. If it took us six months to develop a medicine and get it certified, we would do it because the larger vision was that we were not doing this for today, we were building for the future. All three of us strongly believed in this.

And there was an implicit understanding that we won't bring it out if we cannot use it even if the certification was in place. The emphasis on product efficacy has been the cornerstone of Gynoveda's success. I don't think it would have worked for us if we had not believed in our products and offerings. There are so many other businesses that Vishal and I could do if we just wanted quicker returns. There was a good reason we chose this business.

The ayurvedic formulations, known as APMs (ayurvedic proprietary medications), are our intellectual property and are produced by multiple manufacturers throughout India. These are all first-generation manufacturers. Vishal and I are motivated by the desire to improve the lives of women. I think the revenue and scale are outcomes that you can't chase without first focusing on how your product offers an effective solution to a problem.

What are the current stats for product sales, turnover and users?
Our present annual revenue run rate is approximately Rs 210 crore. Five years since inception, we are close to a 400-member team, and, most importantly, we are a profitable business. I believe that was what made the investors pay attention and eat out of our hands.

What is your vision for Gynoveda?
We want to be the first choice when it comes to advice and products about fertility and women's health. At this point in time, we are relevant to couples who are looking for natural conception and women in the age group of 15 to 55 for their menstrual and reproductive health. Our first ayurveda fertility clinic was launched in Malad, Mumbai, in October 2023 and by 31 March 2025 we had 35 clinics across India.

We are looking to expand to over 300 clinics in the next three years. The clinic business is centred around three A's—authenticity, accessibility and affordability. Our tagline, '*Gynoveda hai, toh good news pakki hai*', reflects our dedication to helping couples who want to have children. With our network of clinics and video consultations, we aim to solve the infertility problems faced by over 30 million couples in India.

There is no greater satisfaction than being able to witness the birth of our precious 'Gynoveda baby' (a term coined by our patients) and we are proud to be celebrating over 20,000 Gynoveda babies.

What would you tell women looking to get into entrepreneurship?
Go for it. Go with the flow.

Honestly, there is too much advice out there. I don't think I took this leap of faith with any fear. And I was fearless because I had lived long enough to know that I would be able to bounce back. Though there was no safety net or Plan B. This was the only plan and it had to succeed. Luck also plays a role, but I haven't seen it around honestly. For women entrepreneurs or anyone who wishes to step beyond of their comfort zone, there is a lovely quotation that comes to mind, 'If not you, then who? If not now, then when?'

This is one of my favourite quotes. This is what had mattered to me because Vishal and I felt so strongly about what we were building that there was no reason for us to wait. Thankfully, somewhere along the way we earned the right to win. What will it grow to? How will we scale? That can be discussed later. But at this point, I doubt I could ever consider doing anything else.

What does a day in your life look like now, as an entrepreneur?
On a typical day I wake up around 6:30 a.m. Chai is my energy booster and *chai pe charcha* with Vishal is my sacred ritual. Both (I hope he does too) of us eagerly look forward to this. I walk for an hour at least four days a week between 7:30 a.m. and 8.30 a.m. and the only accessory I need while I walk is my favourite Bollywood workout playlist. And then it is one hour non-stop walking. Over a period of time, I have realized that walking helps clear my mind and gets me prepped for the day ahead. I avoid checking my work-related emails and WhatsApp messages until 9 a.m. Along with intermittent fasting, I am trying my best to stick to my digital detox between 9 p.m. and 9 a.m. I am glad to report I have been fairly successful in this endeavour. I have a healthy, home-cooked breakfast by 9:30 a.m. and then I am off to work.

A typical day begins at 10:30 a.m., the first half of the day is reserved for what 'I' need to achieve. My energy levels are at its peak in the first half. I can think better and so this time is for strategic planning and getting my game plan ready for what needs to be done in the day and the week. The second half is for team meetings, reviews and brainstorming sessions, which is loaded with people and ideas. At least two days a week, I hold webinars with team members (as we are now a team size of over 400) scattered across India as a personal connect is very much needed. I am now able to wind up on most days at 7 p.m. and it is a blessing that home is just 10 minutes away from the workplace. Evenings are complete down time, with undivided attention to the teen (not sure if he reciprocates wholly) and dinner usually before 8 p.m.

Over the years, I have mastered the art of switching off. It has taken me a while to get to this stage, but thankfully I am able to practise this now without any guilt. Once I am home, I am in the domestic goddess zone and with full DND mode on. The two aspects that I feel describe my typical day and what I thrive on are that I am a sucker for daily routine and consistency.

10

"Change doesn't happen by waiting for the demand of a product—it happens by creating it"

Rashi Sanon Narang
Founder and Creative Director,
Heads Up For Tails

The story of Heads Up For Tails (HUFT) begins with a puppy—Sara, a dog gifted to Rashi Sanon Narang for her 24th birthday. A lifelong pet lover, Rashi's husband decided to surprise her with a dog, and that moment would go on to change everything. Sara not only stole Rashi's heart but also ignited a spark that would eventually become HUFT, a company dedicated to creating high-quality products for pets. This was the beginning of Rashi's entrepreneurial journey, one that took root in 2008, working from a spare room in her home in Delhi.

Rashi's journey was anything but easy. A girl from Delhi who pursued a BBA at Cardiff University and later studied Human Resource Management at the London School of Economics, Rashi's career was far removed from the pet care industry. After working at Citigroup in human resources, she moved to New York with her husband, only to return to India when his job brought them back. It was during this time that Sara entered her life, and with her, the seed for HUFT was planted. Frustrated by the lack of quality pet products, Rashi decided to take matters into her own hands. She began to explore ways to create products that would not only meet the needs of pets but also help change the way people viewed their furry friends.

With limited savings and a few small loans from family, Rashi took her first steps into the pet care industry, a market that was practically non-existent at the time. After facing rejection from over 200 businesses, Rashi pivoted and took her products directly to the customers, setting up pop-up stalls during Diwali and Christmas exhibitions. In 2009, she rented a tiny kiosk in Saket Mall, Delhi, investing just Rs 5 lakh. This kiosk became the heart of her business—a place where she could interact directly with other pet parents, understand their needs and refine her products based on real-world feedback.

In 2009, Rashi's life took another turn when her husband's job transferred them to Singapore. Running a business remotely was difficult, especially in an industry where logistics and supply chains were practically non-existent. Yet, Rashi remained determined.

She proceeded to create HUFT remotely with a small staff of just 10 individuals while juggling work and personal obligations as a new mother. Despite the distance, Rashi never lost sight of her mission to create quality products for pets and change the way people viewed pet care.

In 2015, Rashi and her husband decided to return to India to take the business to the next level. After her spouse became a full-time partner, they set out to make HUFT a significant force in the pet care sector. During her time in Singapore, Rashi also connected with investors, leading to her first round of investment from Singapore-based investors and high-net-worth individuals. In 2019, the company completed a $10 million Pre-Series A funding round, and by 2021,

HUFT raised Rs 277 crore in funding from Verlinvest, Sequoia Capital India, Amitell Capital, and existing investors, including W&C PetTech.

With more than 100 stores and spas spread across 18 cities, including Delhi, Mumbai, Bengaluru, Chennai, Hyderabad, Ahmedabad and Lucknow, HUFT has expanded from its modest beginnings to become a Rs 290-crore corporation. In addition to its strong retail footprint, HUFT boasts a thriving online presence, with an e-commerce website and an app serving customers across India. Today, the brand is the leading choice for pet parents searching for anything from toys and treats to clothing and bedding for their pets.

But for Rashi, the mission has always been greater than just selling products. It is about helping people understand that their pets are family. This shift in perspective has driven HUFT's success, with the company fostering a culture where pets are not merely animals—they are cherished family members. Through the HUFT Foundation, Rashi has ensured that the company's success is also reflected in its commitment to social responsibility, with initiatives supporting street animals, promoting Indie dog pride and raising funds for animal shelters through campaigns like India's largest dogathon.

HUFT has also become a pioneer in sustainability, integrating eco-friendly initiatives into the brand's core. The company is focused on making a positive environmental impact, from upcycled products made with recycled PET(rPET) to replacing plastic packaging with honeycombed cardboard strips. They have even introduced flushable cat litter made from recycled newsprint, ensuring that sustainability is as integral to their ethos as their commitment to quality pet care.

From a one-woman operation to a brand with nearly 1,500 employees, HUFT is a leader in the pet care space. The company's products are designed with care, keeping in mind the specific needs—like a water bowl for cocker spaniels that keeps their long ears out of the water and orthopaedic beds for aging dogs. One of the brand's most beloved products is Sara's Treats, named after the very dog who inspired it all. Made from human-grade ingredients, these treats are preservative-free, hormone-free and antibiotic-free, embodying Rashi's commitment to quality and care. HUFT's entire range of food and treats is made in their world-class innovation and manufacturing centre, with a commitment to excellence at its core.

HUFT kept innovating even during the pandemic, launching toys that gave dogs stuck indoors much-needed mental stimulation and a dog sanitizer for their paws. Rashi's keen interest in pet psychology and her unwavering desire to enhance the lives of pets and their owners are reflected in products like lick mats to stimulate dogs' senses, snuffle mats for enjoyable mealtimes, and yakies chew bones to soothe nervous dogs.

Rashi's journey has been nothing short of remarkable. Hard work and dedication have earned her the recognition of being named Brand of the Year at the World Branding Awards four times. In 2023, she was also honoured with the Woman Ahead award at the Economic Times Startup Awards. Despite many challenges, Rashi remains motivated by her deep love for the mission she set out on—not just creating products that enhance pets' lives but helping pet parents understand their pets better, ensuring every furry companion is treated as a cherished member of the family.

Her story is a testament to the power of passion, perseverance and purpose—proof that when you follow your heart, you can turn a simple idea into a movement that changes the way the world sees its pets.

Excerpts from a conversation over a call in October 2023:

Tell us a bit about your childhood, your family, your growing years and your influences. Were you introduced to entrepreneurship in any way during your childhood?

From a young age, I had a deep connection with animals. Whether it was the street cats wandering in and out of our house, or the dogs playing in our neighbourhood, or even the butterflies and birds that caught my attention, I would spend hours observing them, rescuing them when they were hurt or in need of care. Taking care of animals was not just my hobby; it was an integral part of my identity.

I grew up in a simple joint family in New Delhi, where the house was always full of energy, laughter and the comforting presence of my family—parents, brothers, grandparents, aunt, uncle and cousins. It was a warm, loving environment, and there was never a dull moment. There were always dogs around!

My parents encouraged me to pursue my passions while instilling the importance of responsibility and hard work. As the only girl in a family full of boys, I was showered with love and attention, which made my childhood quite special. I had a sheltered childhood. While I wasn't very extroverted, I formed close, meaningful friendships along the way. I found great joy in art and music.

Despite my quiet nature, I always had a keen interest in entrepreneurship. It started with small ventures like selling handmade cards during Diwali, creating tiny libraries for the neighbourhood kids, organizing community fairs to raise funds for animal charities. The thrill wasn't in the money; it was in the joy of creating something with purpose. Even at a young age, I knew I wanted to make an impact.

My two passions—animals and entrepreneurship—were quietly shaping my future. I was a dreamer, often imagining a life full of possibilities—becoming an astronaut, a vet, or even a geologist working with National Geographic. But life had its own plans. Though my love for animals led me towards the sciences, the thought of animal dissections turned me away, and I eventually gravitated towards design. Yet, nothing felt quite right.

I settled on the practical route by studying commerce and later pursuing a business degree with a master's in human resources. Soon after, I landed a job at a multinational bank through campus placement. But on day three, I knew this wasn't where I was meant to be. Despite the excitement of the prestigious job, sitting at my desk in a massive office with thousands of people, I couldn't shake off the feeling that my work didn't matter. There was a quiet voice in my head saying, 'This isn't my calling.'

After getting married, I moved to my husband's home. I left my job and began exploring different interests—working with an NGO, connecting with children and finding a sense of purpose in new ways. But then, a little puppy named Sara entered my life, and everything changed.

Though my husband's family had never had a dog, he surprised me with one for my birthday. Slowly but surely, Sara captured everyone's heart. For the first time, I was a pet parent, responsible for every decision, from her food and treats to her bedding and toys. It was a profound shift—I was no longer the child of the house, but the caregiver of this little soul.

On Sara's first birthday, I set out to find her a special gift, but nothing felt worthy of her. The shampoos were loaded with chemicals, the biscuits overly processed and the toys lacked heart—everything seemed artificial and uninspired. I couldn't help but wonder *how can I help her live her best life with these products?* That moment ignited something deep inside me. I made a promise to myself—I would create something better, not just for Sara, but for all pets and their parents who craved high-quality, thoughtfully crafted products.

In the months that followed, I started researching—about pets, about ingredients of pet food, about the fabrics and styles that could bring my ideas to life. But there was a challenge: the pet market was barely even a market. Let alone capturing it! There were practically no players in it, and there was no data to guide me. Vendors were uninterested, even offended at the idea of making products for dogs and cats. But I refused to give up. I started small by creating soft furnishings and bedding products because that felt like the right place to begin.

This was back in 2008. Pet stores existed, but they were basic—selling only biscuits and balls. With a small collection of products, I eagerly approached store owners, to share something new and unique. But the response was discouraging. They strongly believed that there were no buyers for such products. They showed me the door, and it stung. Yet, in hindsight, I understood. These were traders, not pet parents. How could they share my vision?

Still, I pressed on. Months later, a store in Bengaluru called Paws responded positively, and they agreed to showcase my products. That was the turning point, and years later, we merged with them, bringing in new partners—Ridhima and Sandeep—who shared the same passion.

Since not many stores were interested in stocking our collections, I had to find another way to reach customers. I began participating in Diwali and Christmas melas/exhibitions, and the response was overwhelmingly positive.

Customers were excited, eager for something new, something that spoke to their needs as pet parents. Those interactions gave me fresh ideas for innovative products. Without even realizing it, I was practising 'design thinking'—using customer feedback to fuel creativity and solve problems.

Through the years, this process of listening and learning has led to the creation of over 200 India-first products, several born from a conversation with a customer. And then, I took a risk. I rented a tiny 100-sq-ft kiosk at Select City Walk, in Delhi. I could not afford the regular rental for a month or a year, so I asked for a two-day rental instead. They agreed, and that small space became the birthplace of something much bigger. It was not just a kiosk; it became a place of hope and passion, where we set out to change perspectives, bringing respect and understanding to how pets should be treated. Seventeen years later, we are still there.

And that was where it all began. Grateful for the chance they gave me, I still look back on that tiny kiosk as the moment when everything shifted—when a dream I had carried for years finally started to take shape.

How did you manage to run the company long distance when you had to relocate to Singapore after your husband got transferred there? Did you at any point think of shutting down, and what kept you going through this?

About a year after I started HUFT, my husband got transferred to Singapore. So, we packed up and moved, and suddenly, I was managing this small fledgling business from thousands of miles away. It was tough. What made it harder was that I had no idea how long we would be there. We ended up staying for seven years. Honestly, I don't know how I managed.

But one thing was clear—no matter how small HUFT was, I wasn't going to let the flame die out. At that time, we had just one point of sale. The webstore would go on and off, depending on whether we could manage stock. I hired a small team—mostly through friends and family—because hiring was difficult. People questioned the pet industry, the career prospects and whether this was even a 'real' business.

So, we got onboard dog and cat lovers who believed in what we were doing. We were young, full of energy and willing to figure things out as we went. It was really just one day at a time.

The next challenge was getting people to even know that we existed. Luckily, social media was just starting to take off. Digital marketing became my way to share our story and introduce people to our products. But communication was hard as this was not the era of Zoom and remote work. I would Skype with my team whenever I could and fly back to India every couple of months to stay connected with them.

That phase was … a lot. We had no funds, a tiny team, no supply chain, no brand awareness and no customers. Everything had to be built from scratch—backend, frontend, expertise and most importantly, trust. I was also a new mother. It was messy, exhausting and overwhelming. But I just went with the flow.

I kept HUFT afloat with my savings—a few lakhs—and small loans from my parents. The other day, I was cleaning my cupboard and found an old cheque book with entries such as 'Rs 50,000—return of loan from Mom & Dad'; 'Rs 20,000—return of loan from Mom & Dad'. The amounts were not huge, but I was determined to pay them back quickly. Sales would trickle in daily or weekly, so every rupee mattered.

No matter how small we were, I woke up every single day with fire in my belly—to do more, to serve my customers, my team, my investors and the community of pets with my whole heart.

In 2016, we finally moved back to India. And with that, a new chapter began.

What were the initial challenges of setting up a business in a completely new space in India?

When I started, there were pet owners in India—but not many had truly discovered the magic of sharing their home and life with a pet. Over the years, I have witnessed the most exquisite transformation take place—pet owners becoming pet parents.

The mindset 'A dog is just a dog' slowly shifted. People began seeing their pets as companions, then as the most wonderful beings in their lives. And finally, as family members—ones they wanted to love, care for and give the finest life to.

This change did not happen overnight. It took time, and there is still a long way to go. But I feel grateful to have witnessed this shift, especially during the pandemic, when people spent more time with their pets and realized just how much joy and love they bring. However, in those early days, we were not just trying to sell products; rather we were in the process of developing something that had never been done before. The problem? If no one had built these products before, clearly there was no demand for them.

Most vendors we approached shut the door on us—some sneering at the thought of making products 'for dogs and cats'. The few who agreed thought it to be a small experiment, not something worth taking seriously. And once we did manage to make products, the majority of the retailers refused to stock them. Additionally, there was resistance to spending on pets. Even when people considered them family, very few wanted to learn about things like good nutrition, quality materials, or why one brand was better than another.

Change doesn't happen by waiting for demand of a product—it happens by creating it. And I am incredibly proud that HUFT worked relentlessly to educate people, to spark conversations, and started a movement in converting pet owners into pet parents. We did not just sell products. We told stories. We shared knowledge. We helped people understand what their pets truly needed, why their health and happiness mattered and how they could provide them the best life possible.

And that is my greatest source of pride. Because change always starts small—but when you believe in it enough, when you work hard enough, it blossoms into something greater than you ever imagined.

What were the initial products in your basket, and how did you expand your offline presence? What were the key learnings while setting up stores and spas for pets as a first mover in this space? When we launched the online store, we barely got any orders because no one was even searching for what we were creating. These products had never existed before in India, so people weren't aware they could exist. We quickly realized that beyond just selling, we had to educate—we had to make our products discoverable and help people understand why their pets needed them.

At the same time, we saw a huge gap in awareness. Pet parents were trying their best, but there was so little information available. We wanted to create a space where we could ask questions, offer advice and guide people in making better decisions for their pets.

Take dog walking, for example. Most people were using choke chains, shock collars, or other aversive tools that had been around for decades. But the truth is, these tools can be extremely harmful. Imagine cutting off a dog's oxygen supply every time they pull on a tool like that—just because they get excited to see a squirrel or chase a smell.

These methods don't just cause immediate discomfort they lead to long-term health issues that often go undiagnosed. We kept asking ourselves: How do we give families the right advice so they can make the best decisions for their pets? How do we help pets live happier, healthier and more comfortable lives?

This was one of the key reasons we decided to go offline. In 2017, we opened our first store in Chhatarpur, New Delhi. It took time to grow, but it gave us something invaluable—direct interaction with pet parents. We could have real conversations, answer questions and build a community.

A few months later, we opened another store. Then another. We experimented with different locations—neighbourhoods, malls, high streets—trying to figure out what worked best. We wanted to be where pet parents were, but also where they felt comfortable spending time with their pets.

We knew we could scale if we found our rhythm. And from then on, we grew with intention, focusing on not just selling products, but building a movement—one that helps pet parents make informed, thoughtful decisions every step of the way.

You raised your first round of funding through high net worth individuals. How did that come about? What were the challenges you faced during fundraising?

We were fortunate to meet some incredible, like-minded individuals who genuinely believed in what we were creating. We raised our angel rounds because we shared a vision that centred on passion for pet care. When it was time for our Series A, we took the step towards venture capital.

Honestly, we have not faced major obstacles in fundraising. There has always been a lot of inbound interest, and I am incredibly grateful for that. But raising capital is not just about securing funds—it is a huge responsibility. You are not just taking money; you are taking on expectations, commitments and the need to scale in the right way.

That is why having the right partners at the right time is so critical. And personally, I could not have done it alone. I have an incredible team, and I rely on them a lot because balancing everything—raising a child and managing my home, my family and the business while also bringing on investors was overwhelming.

Taking on investment is a serious decision, one that requires clarity, alignment and an immense sense of responsibility. And I have learned that for things to truly work out, the right partnerships make all the difference.

You have also set up the HUFT Foundation. Tell us about its mission and the motivation behind its creation?

The HUFT Foundation is incredibly close to my heart. We share our neighbourhoods with so many animals—this is their home too. Yet, there is often conflict instead of coexistence, and we really want to change that. Our goal is to shift mindsets, to encourage compassion and peaceful living alongside these animals, rather than seeing them as a nuisance.

Through the foundation, we try to make a tangible difference with initiatives like feeding drives, reflective collar campaigns, adoption events and vaccination drives. Beyond that, we strongly believe in the power of education. When people understand animal welfare—when they learn about kindness, responsibility and respect for all living beings—they are more likely to act and create a positive impact.

Over time, we aspire to create a more compassionate world—one where people see street animals not as 'strays' but as part of the community, and where humans and the natural world can thrive together in harmony.

What are your most popular products?
Right now, our most popular products are treats—especially our all-natural range, which pet parents love because they are clean, healthy and made with real ingredients.

We have also launched our first food product, Sara's Wholesome Food, named after my dog, Sara, who inspired HUFT. We have poured our whole heart into this—ensuring it is packed with high-quality nutritious ingredients to truly benefit every dog who eats it. It is truly a world-class product, and is fast becoming one of our bestselling items, and that means the world to us.

Toys are another fast-moving category, as pet parents are always looking for ways to keep their dogs engaged, active and happy. We love seeing how our products bring joy to pets and their families!

What is your typical day like?

My days are long, full and deeply fulfilling. I start early to get my daughter ready for school, which is always a special time. After that, I treasure a quiet morning to myself with my doggies by my side, a cup of chai, and a moment to read, journal and reflect. A walk in the park follows, grounding me before the whirlwind of the day begins.

Once I am at work, the hours fly by, filled with passion, purpose and endless tasks. I love what I do, and that keeps me energized. My evenings are spent relaxing, spending time with my family, my doggies and my loved ones—unwinding, sharing moments and managing home.

Some days are overwhelming, some are tough and some just flow beautifully. But I have learned that even the hardest days bring lessons, and I try to embrace them with gratitude. And of course, I celebrate the good seasons when they come!

I prefer to manage my time intentionally—I plan my week every Sunday, ensuring that the most important things, both at work and in my personal life, are scheduled. Because what gets scheduled, gets done! And just as I make time for work, I make time for myself—to stay inspired, to dream and to hold on to the vision that keeps me moving forward.

Finally, what is your vision for Heads Up For Tails?
At HUFT, our vision is simple yet profound—we want every home to enjoy having pets as members of the family.

I have witnessed the incredible transformation that happens when people share their homes and lives with animals. They become more empathetic, more kind, more compassionate—and in many ways, they become better people. If we could help everyone become the best versions of themselves through their relationship with their pets, I believe the world would be such a lovely place.

I want people to truly understand their pets, so we can help them live their best lives. Pets are magical creatures, and we are here to serve them in the best way we know how, with love, care and dedication.

11

"[W]hen you empower a woman, you empower her entire ecosystem"

Ridhi Doongursee
Co-Founder, Lxme

Building a tech company was probably the last thing on Ridhi Doongursee's mind when she was a young girl growing up in Mumbai. She is one of two daughters born into a Marwari household that is both modern and yet traditional in other aspects. But after much persuasion her parents allowed young Ridhi to go to the UK to study at Warwick as an undergrad student, even though they had no family in the country and Ridhi would be on her own for the first time.

Ridhi was a sensible and practical young girl, and more importantly, very ambitious. She worked odd jobs during her undergrad years and landed an internship and eventually a job at UBS (formerly known as Union Bank of Switzerland) after graduating with a Bachelor of Science and Business Studies.

But after a while, the strain and loneliness of being alone abroad took a toll on her and Ridhi decided to return to her family in India. She joined the family business, got married and became a serial entrepreneur by establishing financial services and supply chain start-ups CreditMonk.com and Industricals.

Ridhi became a co-founder of Lxme alongside Priti Rathi Gupta, who had set it up as a Facebook community initially before expanding to an app. Ridhi is a strong advocate for women's financial empowerment and brings over 15 years of experience in financial services, fintech and e-commerce along with her start-up background. With the knowledge and steep learning curve associated with building start-ups, Ridhi has mastered the art of efficiently creating and growing businesses with the resources and talent at hand.

Lxme is India's first financial platform for women. What began as a Facebook community in 2020 by Priti Rathi Gupta, the app now has over eight lakh women subscribers and is growing at an impressive pace. By integrating literacy, payments, wealth management and lending features into a single app, the platform's ultimate goal is to assist women in efficiently and effectively managing all their finances.

When she is not helping women get a grip on managing their money and investments, Ridhi is managing a household with two children, her husband and three pets. She is also an author of a book on parenting titled *7 Steps to Loving More and Worrying Less.* Ridhi is a music enthusiast as well as a foodie and loves to travel with her family. But now her full attention is on her latest baby, Lxme. She is eager to watch it develop into a behemoth while empowering Indian women to take charge of their finances and make them financially astute.

Excerpts from an interview conducted in Mumbai in December 2023:

Tell us about your childhood, your family and your influences growing up? What was it like being the first girl from a conservative family to study abroad?

I was born and raised in Mumbai in the 1980s in a Marwari household, which was very traditional and protective in some respects and quite modern in others. I never wanted my parents to feel the gap for not having a boy since they had two daughters. As a result, I became this person who wanted to achieve, build and prove. And somehow, I convinced my family to send me to England for Grade 12.

It was hard to break that mindset initially since I was the first in the family to do so. The expectations were high because the choice was not normal so I had to prove myself more than I would have ordinarily. I went to Stratford for my Grade 12, then I went to Warwick for undergrad where I did a double degree in computer science and business. I also performed a variety of odd jobs. I loved working. It was a great learning experience—from living with a host family during my Grade 12 to working odd jobs to giving my best to my academics. Whether it was obtaining the greatest callbacks for telesales or stocking shelves at Marks & Spencer, my part-time employment allowed me a unique perspective on life. From mastering the regional accents and dialects to being fortunate enough to be selected for an internship with UBS London, I learned a lot about living independently which also moulded me as a person.

While I missed home, I couldn't turn down the amazing offer from UBS London to work there full-time when I graduated. The opportunity of working in London, the whole job experience, and the fact that they were handling my visa were all too alluring to pass up. So, I stayed back.

Why did you decide to return to India and how did you then decide to become an entrepreneur instead of entering the corporate world? Tell us about your two previous businesses CreditMonk and Industricals.

I always missed India, family and friends so I did want to come back, but I was certain that I wanted to get some work experience, so I completed a little over a year at UBS. I was keen to join my family business and expand it because I never wanted to make my parents feel the absence of a son.

I worked in the family business for a while and then I got married. While one side of the business was pretty much set up and established and the other side was being set up, I realized early on that I like being part of a growth story.

Considering my varied experience and love for building, I set up their online presence and internal digitization and then I realized that there are certain critical problems that businesses in India always face, and a lot of those can get solved with technology. That was when I began my journey in the start-up ecosystem, and set up CreditMonk.

An easy way to describe it is that it was a TripAdvisor for businesses. Small- and medium-scale businesses in India all work on credit and the sad reality is that nobody pays on time. Every small or medium businessman spends most of his time chasing delayed payments. I was thinking of a way to solve this. This was around the time of a major scandal involving a jeweller. The banks had debt with him, but nobody in the diamond markets had debt with him because they knew about the risks involved.

Everyone in the closed ecosystem was in the know about whom you could give credit to and not. I wanted to democratize that information. Your CIBIL score and bank statement serve as your primary proof of your ability to repay a loan, followed by your intention to do so.

So the focus of CreditMonk was to rate the intention to pay and the market reputation of a company or a business, which others entering into business dealings with them could refer to before they began. There is already offline business lending between friends and between businesses—a Marwari lends to a Marwari, a Gujarati borrows from a Gujarati and a person in the diamond business lends to another person in the same business. B2B lending was the method used to monetize the entire credit rating market. The portal rates payment habits of businesses. Its main aim is to make credit a good word by enabling business owners to review and rate payment habits of businesses that they have dealt with. This makes companies publicly accountable and facilitates a foolproof way to assess a company's payment habit before dealing with them or extending them credit.

We developed the algo, we were one of the first to build out the Aadhar APIs; GST had not launched. We had a very small tight team. But then the regulators came out with a white paper that restricted P2P (peer-to-peer) lending, making our idea of a business-to-business platform unviable for the time being.

My silent partner at the time was setting up Industricals, a B2B platform for electricals, hardware and home improvement supplies.

He asked me to take over to build India's first B2B retail distribution online platform for property improvement supplies and that was how Industricals 2.0 started. We set up across Mumbai around five years ago.

How did your partnership with Priti Rathi Gupta to co-found Lxme come about?
Though Industricals had survived the pandemic, external funding was not easy to get. In order to find a compromise between managing

dilution and obtaining finance, one of us had to stand aside, and Industricals was incorporated into the partner's main business.

Around that time, I met Priti and discussed opportunities to work together. Naturally, my interest in fintech and finance remained a major factor in the direction I was taking. When I heard what Lxme wanted to do I could instantly relate to it, both technologically as well as from a woman's perspective.

Priti's vision that every woman should have access to wealth management was something that resonated with me. Creating a trusted platform for women to explore regulated investment options in a fair, mature and transparent manner was something that I also believed was a huge opportunity.

At that time, as much as the business, I think it was the building of a partnership between two individuals that became our focus. There is the saying that being a co-founder is like a marriage. And I think that applies as much to our case as it does in most successful business partnerships. Given the amount of time we spend together, Priti and I have reached an innate understanding of each of our strengths and have deep trust and respect for each other.

Our joint vision for Lxme is also what drives us. Lxme is not an initiative; it is a revolution to transform the relationship women have with money and is built to be a successful, scalable and profitable business. It is India's first full-stack financial platform for women.

Why did you decide to focus on women investors? What have your learnings been about this category of consumers of financial products? How much education has been needed? What holds this consumer back from taking charge of her finances?

Priti started it as a community first. It was born from her expertise and deep interest in financial services and identifying the gap in the market where women were not being specifically catered to. She wanted women to have financial literacy and access to investment tools from the formative stages of their lives as true equality is incomplete without financial independence. Women should take charge of her financial goals and be an equal contributor to the family's financial decisions.

That sort of set the tone for the app. We did community, we did literacy and then we did curated investment portfolios. Women are super smart and diligent. They are ready to put in any amount of work and they are highly aspirational. So, if you make them feel safe, they will. And obviously for us also, there is constant learning. We focus on education, support and communication. Our target market's perception of our offerings has been greatly influenced by the openness and truthfulness of our product information.

We also quickly discovered the paradox of women—they are masters at managing a household-monthly budget but afraid to grow the pie. Overall, we have learnt that women are more risk aware rather than risk averse and therefore make only cautious choices.

Prior to beginning, we conducted a survey of women and money power and interviewed a few thousand women. We found that 95 per cent of women regardless of whether from Tier 1 or Tier 2 cities, whether married or unmarried, had children or not, were employed or not, did not access any financial news or financial services platform. However, 76 per cent said they would love to if it was made relatable to them. Surprisingly, women in Tier 2 were investing more than those in Tier 1.

This also then gave us the opportunity to address this audience through language support and localization support and build this into the app. This is all part of the trust we build through the overall digital experience.

Given the growing number of women in the workforce and the general increase in women's empowerment, we believe that now is the ideal moment to advance financial literacy and investing.

What would you tell women entrepreneurs about decision-making when it comes to their enterprises?

I believed that each of my start-ups was *the one!* Naturally, every entrepreneur thinks that and that is the key motivator that drives its creation. I gave Industricals my everything. But every decision has to be taken with an end goal in mind and when that goal post keeps moving, experience and good judgement come into play. Speaking to peers, friends, family to get their views always helps. It is also crucial to build a network of people who offer an unbiased viewpoint. Ultimately, every decision is measured and in the best interest of the business and my future involvement with it.

What are the unique offerings on the platform?

We have over 70,000 members on Facebook, over 8,00,000 on our app, and more on all of our other social media platforms. Everything on the app is curated for women. Our women-only community is a safe space to talk and get support from experts. We have a one-hour financial fitness bootcamp that helps you with all the critical aspects of personal finance with simple steps to start immediately. It is a fun, gamified and simplified version of financial literacy.

Additionally, unique non-financial power features like a vision board that connects to calculators and steps to achieve your goals, a savings challenge to help you develop a savings habit and a financial security quiz, to name a few.

Women love the community as they feel safe there though some are quiet and just observe reading everyone's questions and answers. That is the one thing that women love—a safe space to ask questions, and the associated behavioural shift that results from financial literacy. And then they move on to the 360-degree money ecosystem that helps them build their financial safety net and a path to achieving their financial goals as well.

How do you envision the platform expanding and impacting more women? Are there any plans to take it globally?
We believe Lxme is headed towards being one of India's biggest money apps because when you empower a woman, you empower her entire ecosystem. Our goal is to empower 20 million Indian women to manage their finances and establish ourselves as the go-to app for all things money within the next five years.

We are frequently asked about the need for a platform like Lxme on a global scale. Financial services is a highly regulated sector and each country has its own regulations. There is tremendous potential for the business but we want to see our full vision translate to reality in India first before we expand to other markets.

What is a typical day in your life like? How do you optimize your time with your family, especially your children?

I have two kids. One is now 17 and the other one is ten. Two kids, three pets, a start-up, a home to run and an incredibly supportive husband. So, while every day is a balancing act, as it is for most working mothers, I am lucky to have the resources and family that allow me to keep both ends balanced. Yes, there are times when my kids feel the gap but they have come to understand that I need to work and building my business contributes to my overall happiness. They are aware that time can occasionally be limited, but love is boundless.

I have become a skilled administrator of life, just as the majority of women have mastered multitasking! Creating schedules, calendars, menus, ensures that what has to tick without my daily intervention, ticks. And on those days when things fall apart, you count your lucky stars that the kids, the husband and the wider ecosystem pick up the pieces if you are not around to do so.

What would you tell women who plan to get into entrepreneurship?
Go for it. You are fabulous. Women are fabulous organizers, they are hardworking, they are honest and they are diligent. Go for it. Be fearless! Just plan your financial commitments and emergency fund in advance.

Women are caregivers, breeders, nurturers and guardians. Instinctively, we are organizers. We are fearless about moving homes and setting up a new life with our husband (and his family), and while it is daunting at first, it soon becomes second nature. I would say the same for creating a business. It is a learning curve as well. I believe that the freedom to be an entrepreneur is invaluable, provided that the fundamental financial management decisions are addressed, such as who will pay the bills and so forth. Creating something and watching it grow through a daily discipline of hard work is extremely rewarding and has been one of my biggest motivators.

Lxme is my passion. The potential is huge, and success is based on a combination of that potential, hard work, some amount of luck and phenomenal teamwork every single day!

12

"We wanted to defy the stereotypes long attached with wearing saris …"

Taniya and Sujata Biswas
Co-Founders,
Suta

A cat sits at the entrance to the Suta office on the first floor of a nondescript industrial estate in Kalina, Mumbai. It is curled up contentedly next to the desk of the security staff and mews indifferently as one passes. The sisters Taniya and Sujata Biswas seem just as comfortable in their own skin. The owners of Suta have started a whole new fashion movement by bringing saris back into style for young Indian women and transforming the clothing from a traditional wedding, festival and religious attire into a stylish everyday item worn by women of all ages.

The cat stretches and decides to walk with you into the office, and once in, it finds itself another corner to curl up in again. Not that this is an office that allows for curling up contentedly. Far from it. The office is full of dynamic energy. There are bales and cartons coming in, fabric wherever you look, and people rushing around with a sense of urgency that has so far completely eluded the cat.

Inside, in a conference room, the Suta sisters, both in their mid-30s, are in the thick of a meeting with their team. Vivacious and dynamic in their individual way, they are both so in sync with each other that they tend to complete one another's thoughts and sentences. They also are, by the luck of the genetic draw, incredibly gorgeous. Given their resources, that definitely helped when they were building their brand, Suta. They became their own brand models, making them the faces of Suta in a way no amount of marketing muscle and push could have done.

Sujata and Taniya brought their irreverent, sensual individual selves to the brand, which helped Suta get noticed quickly (and how!) making girls and young women realize that saris can, in fact, be sexy, stylish and trendy, and most importantly they can be worn every day, at any time.

It all began, perhaps, back in their childhood, when their mother wore soft well-worn saris at home. They grew up across much of east India, including West Bengal, Bihar, Jharkhand, Vishakhapatnam before finally settling down in Bhubaneswar, Odisha. The older of the two, Sujata who graduated from College of Engineering and Technology (CET), Bhubaneswar, and Indian Institute of Foreign Trade (IIFT), Delhi, went on to work with the Essar Group and Jindal Group. But her heart was not in the corporate world, and she decided to sign up for a PhD in e-commerce at IIT Bombay, hoping to explore how e-commerce is evolving in India and how she can help with social development.

Sujata would eventually give up on the PhD, and instead get down to actually setting up a venture that would create an impact in the D2C space. Taniya graduated in ceramic engineering from NIT Rourkela, got placed at Tata Refractories Ltd, where she worked for a year and then pursued a management degree from IIM Lucknow. She worked for four years in IBM as a strategy consultant after that.

The two sisters had made Mumbai their home, and even as they were in the rough and tumble of the corporate world, the itch to create something of their own was becoming all-consuming. After work, they would sit over chai at home and often wonder whether they should open a pancake chain. The ideas were plenty, but zeroing in on saris took time. Actually, it all began when they would spend time with weavers at nearby villages during school vacations back home.

Or perhaps it began with a venture to showcase Taniya's photography skills on social media in order to get photography assignments. But when they started getting more enquiries for the saris than the photographs, they began creating saris. Their love for saris and their desire to make it an everyday trendy garment eventually morphed into Suta. The name Suta came about serendipitously. It is a combination of the first two letters of their names, and it also means thread, which is consistent with what they have been creating, and interestingly, it also means child, which ties it all together even more beautifully.

They launched Suta in 2016 from Sujata's one-bedroom house with a combined capital of Rs six lakh, pooling in three lakh each as co-founders. The brand began with a single-colour mulmul sari with the aim of creating absolutely simple designs in the best possible quality. They had two weavers and one employee. Today they have over 300 employees and 17,000 artisans all over India, with women making up over 60 per cent of these.

By using social media as their major sales channel, they also disrupted the conventional strategy of promoting their goods through mainstream media. They started with Facebook and then quickly adapted to Instagram, where they have over nine lakh followers today. With a turnover of Rs 75 crore in 2024, they hope to touch the milestone of Rs 100 crore in the next couple of years.

Suta is one of the most sought-after sari brands with young women between the age group of 18–35 years forming their core base. These women would often have to make do with their mother's saris for special occasions, and these saris would not be the ones they would choose for themselves. Suta has closed the gap by creating saris especially for such young women.

The brand which redefined how contemporary urban women in India wore saris, contemporizing the garment and making it sexy, fun and hip at the same time, has many fans among the Indian diaspora too. The Suta Queens, as they call their brand ambassadors, are a devout lot who are known to enthusiastically champion the brand and its ethos. Minimalistic styles and saris, chic blouses, easy price points, all have contributed to making Suta popular among the young and the stylish.

The brand has appeared in movies, OTT series and fashion events. From a completely online presence, the company now has its own stores in Mumbai, Thane, Bengaluru, Hyderabad, Kolkata, Chennai, Bhubaneswar, Pune, Kochi, Trivandrum, Raipur and Delhi with more in the pipeline.

Suta has diversified from saris to blouses, to men's and women's ready-to-wear, to kids', home linen and lifestyle accessories. The Biswas sisters have begun looking at traditional marketing and branding to build the brand. Although they haven't tried their hand at fundraising, they wouldn't rule it out just yet.

The journey to build Suta has seen them bagging a slew of awards, including Indian MSME Woman Entrepreneur of The Year (Small Businesses), Indian Achievers' Award for Young Entrepreneur, Best E-commerce Start-up, Best Emerging Enterprise Enabling Employment in India and many more. They even made it to the Business World 40 under 40 list.

Excerpts from an interview held in March 2023:

Tell us a bit about your growing years and your memories of the sari as a garment from back then. I read something about the comfort of saris drying on the clothesline that you both say are an integral part of childhood memories.

Taniya Biswas (TB): Our father, who is retired now, worked with the Indian Railways. Since he worked for the South Eastern Railways, we were not only in Odisha but also in Bihar, Vizag, Jharkhand, West Bengal, and most of eastern India. One of our favourite memories is of our summer holidays which were spent visiting our relatives in Bengal. We loved wrapping ourselves around saris hanging out to be dried on the line. Those wet, unstarched saris smelt a certain way. We would wear a sari for every festival and important occasion through our childhood and adolescence. Saraswati Puja was one such occasion where we would invariably be draped in a saris.

Sujata Biswas (SB): It was customary to wrap ourselves in a sari on Saraswati Puja. We have photographs of us wearing saris even when we were in Grade 1 or 2. Taniya would wear it with a top and I wore it mostly with a kurta. Growing up, wearing saris became a daily affair because Mom would always wear soft, unstarched saris at home. We would wear the ones she had discarded after long use.

TB: These saris provided us with a certain level of comfort. You could simply wipe your hands on them if you wanted to, but you couldn't do that with a crisp starched sari or a silk sari. We used to love that softness. One of our fondest memories is of Mom bustling around the house wearing her sari with her pallu tucked in the waist. We used to hang those saris on our four-poster bed, transforming it into a tent-like space where we would merrily play. Saris were integral to almost everything that we did.

SB: I have hardly seen Ma wear something other than a sari. Saris have always been part of my childhood memories. Whenever I would get really stressed, I would sit and fold saris. That was therapy for me. As a child, I had folded many saris because they would be lying around occupying a lot of space. It is comforting to make sure that all the lines are together.

TB: When you are young, wearing a sari to a place where people don't wear them very often, like pubs and malls, is a lot of fun.

SB: Wearing a sari will definitely turn heads. It has even got us entry into restaurants without making any reservations! People have challenged this! I tell them, 'Come with me and see.'

You both come from an engineering background, how did you get into the fashion industry? And how did you launch a sari brand that had never been sold online?

SB: Both of us are engineer-MBAs, but before stepping into management, Taniya worked with the Tatas after finishing her engineering. Around the same time, she was selected by top business schools as well as NID, eventually choosing IIM Lucknow. Creativity has always been at the heart of our journey, both of us have loved painting and creating things since the beginning.

TB: Since we studied home science in school, we knew how to stitch a petticoat, how to stitch a salwar kameez and how to stitch a kid's outfit.

SB: Hence Taniya applied for both design and CAT. She cleared both but she chose to pursue an MBA from IIM Lucknow because I had an MBA degree.

TB: For me there was no choice because my sister was someone I looked up to. I knew no one with a design background in my entire *khandan,* so I had no one I could reach out to. In our childhood, we used to play games of making something and selling them, so we knew we would make something and sell it but we didn't know what.

SB: I arrived in Mumbai in 2009 and Taniya joined me after finishing her MBA. I was married by then. I got married in 2013. When Taniya moved to Mumbai, we were living in a one BHK. My husband and I shared a bedroom and a curtain divided the living room, with a bed behind it, and that was Taniya's bedroom.

TB: The corporate life wasn't bad, we enjoyed what we were doing ...

SB: But we were evolving into something else; I sensed that this was not inherently us. My job promotions were regular and good, the salary was decent but that was it, full stop. I was turning into something I wasn't, people were getting scared of me. I was in a very senior position so I had to behave in a certain way that was not nice. So, I quit and decided to do my PhD in a space that interested me. It was while I was pursuing my doctorate, I realized that it was not me. I would teach, I thought maybe, but that also was not me, it wouldn't be very rewarding.

We still didn't know what it was that we really wanted to do; what was it that would really make us feel fulfilled. Taniya is fond of cooking, so first we thought we would open a pancake franchise. We even went hunting for places in Bandra where we could possibly open the first outlet.

TB: And we did a lot of research, from physical research to speaking to people, to understanding how much investment is required, etc. But that made us realize that it was not viable, I could not see any purpose there. I mean feeding people is all good but I'm not going to be happy in the kitchen cooking, that's not what I wanted to end up doing.

SB: Finally, we took a call and decided to do nothing about the pancake chain. We decided to open a photography page because Taniya likes photography and both of us could travel and do photo shoots of weddings, pre-weddings, etc. But then we thought, why get stuck with someone else's schedule? They don't get up on time, they don't start the wedding on time and we are like stuck till late. We reasoned that it would be safer to begin photo shoots of products—people would just provide us with the stuff, and we would take pictures.

TB: So we began doing product shoots for NGOs. We did it for free, firstly to build our portfolio and also because it gave us a certain purpose. But while we were doing that, we discovered that no one was providing us clothes to be shot. We did a lot of jewellery shoots, and shoots for the non-profit company I Was a Sari, which made products from used saris. Then we decided to make a few dresses because we simply loved clothes.

We made pocket dresses and pants with the intention of using them for product photography as part of our portfolio. We would shoot these dresses in different ways in various settings, including outdoors, indoors and in natural light. And we would end up wearing these clothes once we were done with the photography.

We got around 15–20 clothes made and did a shoot with them. But when we sent the photographs out, we got enquiries not for the shoot, but for the clothing. We even managed to sell those clothes, and we kept getting enquiries and they did not stop. And very soon nobody was asking us about the photo shoots, but everybody was asking about the clothes. By then we had done a lot of brand shoots, and the purpose was never clear. What were we doing this for? Was it for only the money?

[*Sujata pauses and reflects.*]

The name Suta came to us through serendipity. And we knew this is it, this is where we should enter, we should do textile.

TB: But we did not like the fabric that was available locally, so we asked our father, who was posted as the assistant commissioner at Howrah in West Bengal, to arrange for a meeting with weavers through his staff members. We thought we could help weavers if we could buy from them. And by doing that, we could assist and collaborate with more people.

With photography, you can build a team of 20 people but how much more can you do? Maybe create a photo agency, but you really can't scale up any further. But we could procure or buy things directly from weavers, or get them to make things specifically for us. No matter how small a number, it was a good place to start.

SB: We actually went on a hunt for fabric but stumbled upon saris. Oh my god, we love saris! And still do. And we decided to use a couple of saris for a shoot.

TB: So, that was how it began. We went looking for fabrics but found saris instead and happily brought them back. It was in Nadia district in West Bengal. Those weavers still work with us, they are a married couple. Initially, many weavers refused to work with us, but this couple agreed. The others either had their own line of business or were supplying to some store or agent. Nobody would agree to work with two young women who knew nothing of the business. But this one couple readily agreed.

[*Taniya pauses and smiles.*]

SB: We began with single-colour mulmul saris, which were pretty much the first saris we shot. We went to Barra Bazar and bought starched mulmul, the ones people used to do handwork on. Me, Taniya, Mom and Dad used to wash it almost 10 times daily to remove the starch and then start selling it.

TB: Since no one wears these saris, we were unable to persuade the weavers to produce them without starch. They would ask us, 'Who are you going to sell these unstarched plain saris to? Widows? Who is going to buy these saris? Are they for a movie, a shoot, a project?' They simply did not understand. Two people gradually came to an agreement, and as the word spread, others joined and the team began to expand. Today we have over 17,000 artisans and weavers working with us and the team strength is of around 300.

Instead of using conventional marketing or advertising, you used social media, particularly Facebook and Instagram, to develop your brand. Was this a deliberate choice?

SB: Initially, Facebook was our main platform. We launched our Facebook page in 2014. And two years later we registered ourselves, but the photography page was called 'As I See'. We then converted it into Suta. Finally in 2017, we joined Instagram.

TB: We wanted to tell the story behind the sari, and we felt that if people related to it they would like the product more and it would be close to their hearts. We wanted our customers to have a strong emotional connection with our products. We didn't want the product to be something you buy, use and throw away. That was the main idea.

SB: And since we couldn't afford models, we would dress in saris and go on photo shoots and try to find different spots within the same house, especially during the lockdown.

TB: Today our marketing team says it is mind-boggling how much time we spent crafting our stories, we could have done SEO instead. [*Taniya laughs aloud.*] We have actually sat down and written the stories behind the products and it has always worked for us. We have just about begun traditional media and advertising because we always retailed online and never really needed it. Now that we are opening stores, we are spending on hoardings and newspaper adverts because traditional brick-and-mortar stores require these.

What were the lessons you learned and the challenges you faced when you first started a business in an industry that was entirely new to you?

TB: Earliest learnings? People laughing at you, conning you, making a fool of you. Also, not knowing how to do business. Initially we thought we would launch easily by asking questions and doing proper research. Although we were quite scared of asking people questions. But when we got duped a few times by vendors, not weavers, mind you, we realized that we cannot reveal our ignorance to them and we can't trust them too much.

Eventually, we figured out that not everyone wants to have a long-term relationship. Some are just interested in making their money from the deal. I think most of them did not expect us to make it this big. They would promise something, show us something and send across something else.

We would pay in advance and then we did not know how to go for lab tests, we just had to trust their word for it. Additionally, I discovered that it was difficult to obtain knowledge on the minor details when we first started showing, even inside our fraternity. When we asked a brand owner for information, they would either ignore us or simply shoo us. No matter how simple the question, they would not assist.

For instance, when we began exhibiting we wanted to get bags printed, and our requirement was only a few, so we asked around where we would get a small quantity of bags printed. When we couldn't find anyone to print our bags, we simply started writing everything with a marker on brown paper bags.

Now we can both do the perfect logo freehand because we did it so many times back then. Information was not so easily available then, and also the printers wanted a quantity of a thousand at least. So, we would just buy the bags and draw the logo ourselves. Now if anyone asks, we are the first people to say, 'Let us help you get it done.'

[*Sujata nods her head vigorously.*]

SB: We know what it feels like to ask when you are starting out and do not have the information or the assistance you need. We host webinars and distribute vendor details. I will even help out another sari business if need be; I will not hesitate because they are our competitor.

I will obviously not share our weaver details because they only work for us but I am happy to help with any other specifics. We know it is so difficult to get good quality advice and new kids on the block struggle.

SB: At the end of the day, the goal is to collaborate with as many weavers as possible. For us, the lack of proper knowledge of textiles was a big hindrance, we had to train ourselves on the job and hit the ground running. We did not do any courses, but after our first designer joined us in 2018, it became a little easier because the designers brought industry knowledge. They were familiar with the jargon. That taught us to ask questions without hesitation, and that was a good learning. Having come from a corporate background, it was quite disheartening to be cheated, some days we would cry.

We would order four metre of cloth and they would send us 3.25 metre, it was so petty sometimes. Once, when we went to a new vendor, we told him, 'You write what you will supply us and sign here.' And he said, *Beta,* it looks like someone has cheated you.' And then he added, 'If you don't trust anyone, your business will not grow. You have to trust.' Just that one piece of advice from him calmed us.

We still work with him. Before that, we were acting like porters. Taniya and I developed blue marks on our shoulders for days because we would carry bales on our shoulders, not trusting the vendors to send us what they had promised.

TB: Since we hailed from a middle-class background, we did not have unlimited resources to dip into. We were spending from our pockets. We had begun with a capital of six lakh, with both of us chipping in three lakh each, which was what we had saved.

Now that the business has scaled up and has reached momentum, are you seeking investors?

SB: Initially we always said no, now we're saying not yet.

TB: You see, we always knew that somewhere down the line we have to open physical stores to fuel the growth. If we have to open 15 stores, we can't be doing it on our own. That is the way we have to think. Is the cost of the money too much? Is diluting our stake worth it? The most important thing in my opinion is that our core vision remains unchanged, and that no one is pushing us to change it .

Suta saris appear to have accomplished the seemingly impossible; they have changed the perception of saris from being totally uncool to trendy and hip, especially among the younger consumers. Saris had almost become ceremonial wear but Suta repositioned it as daily wear. Was this something you deliberately set about trying to create?

SB: Although we did not take any specific steps in that approach, we wanted it to become a staple for the youngsters. We wanted people to know that saris could be worn in a lot of different ways, and that saris were cool. When we had started, Taniya was 25 and I was 27, we assumed that our target market would comprise people in our age group. We never imagined older women would like them too. Because my mother would often say, 'Who will wear a sari without a border? Why is it so *pat pat?* Where's the starch?' And as for younger girls, we never even thought about it.

But then after two years, we discovered that the 18 to 25 age group was our second-largest consumer base. I think we were working in that direction without even realizing it. Young people got drawn to our brand because it was positioned as youthful, vibrant and fuss-free. The price points were reasonable for them. So many girls tell me that they used their pocket money to buy their first sari from Suta. This group was the segment that always borrowed saris from their mothers, aunts, grandmothers, and the saris were not always to their taste. They looked elderly when they wore those saris. How could they wear it with a crop top?

One always picked the good saris from one's mothers, and those needed to be starched, pleated and draped in a certain way. After seeing our saris, I think they realized that they could pick their own saris, wear them a lot, look sexy, turn heads and receive a ton of compliments. Not just look cool but join us in creating a huge impact. We have got so many people who have told us that everyone else at some event or function wore some of India's biggest brands, and they wore a simple Suta sari and still stood out amongst everyone. We had a girl telling us she wore a simple purple sari with a yellow blouse and everyone was talking about her sari and enquiring about the brand. Many among them even recognized it as a Suta sari. We have many such good testimonials. Our customers make their own decisions. Their family would not allow them to wear something like this, for, say, a wedding function. Imagine wearing a sari worth Rs 3,000 for such an occasion! But our clientele decides for themselves.

TB: Suta has gained popularity in Bollywood. The lead actress has worn a Suta in *Rocket Boys;* Pooja Bhatt is wearing one in *Bombay Begums,* and they are all women calling the shots in the shows. Even in the new series *Aap Jaisa Koi,* Fatima Sana Shaikh wore so many Suta saris. The first-ever Suta sari in Bollywood was worn by Kiara Advani in *Lust Stories,* and it was absolutely amazing how she pulled it off.

Did being the faces for Suta help in changing the perception of the sari? What was the strategy behind that?

SB: Initially, we would crop the heads off of all our photos, but this one time Taniya kept my face and said, 'Next time apply a bit of kajal' and it stayed.

TB: After that, we began applying kajal and lipstick and taking our pictures; even today Sujata wears only kajal and lipstick for the shoots. Usually, you don't wear a lot of makeup when you go out, and our saris are like that. We wanted to position our saris like that so our photos had to be relatable and we couldn't have heavy makeup or hair done.

SB: Recently, 15–20 girls were wearing Suta at a college function. I got a picture from a B-school where half the girls were wearing Suta exclusively. Many of our customers send us their pictures and videos when they get together and this wonderful thing has emerged just because we share a love for saris. In the US too, there are a lot of Suta meets that happen. Women just gather wearing Suta saris and have meet-ups. We wanted Suta saris to become regular wear and revive the culture of wearing saris everywhere. Especially these soft breathable saris.

We don't want you to think that saris are difficult to wear. Or what do you pair it with? Wear it with anything. I have three petticoats that I wear with almost all my saris, it doesn't matter. You can wear anything, with anything, it is just a petticoat, even if it is peeping out it is okay. How does it matter? We wanted to make the sari fuss-free and have people stop thinking that they have to be worn in a certain way. I have seen that happening with our mother and her generation that everything needs to be matched. There are no such rules any more.

If you are comfortable with the material/fabric, you can easily manage it through the day, and the sari won't come undone. If you are wearing a comfortable fabric you can wear it all day, go to the office and even attend a party, or a wedding in the same sari. We wanted to defy the stereotypes long attached with wearing saris and so introduced blouses that made saris more fun. Youngsters loved that the most. We came up with the idea when we saw an old lady wearing a sari with a shirt, her son's probably. It was very hip. She looked gorgeous in that. People have been doing this forever; it is just that we have restricted ourselves recently.

Earlier in our corporate avatar, whenever we would wear our mom's saris people would pay us compliments and ask, 'Is there something special today? Are you going to the mandir? Are you going to meet a guy?' Such remarks would make me wonder why people considered wearing a sari meant it was a special day. We should be wearing saris every day. In our office, women often wear saris; it is casual wear for us.

TB: We want foreigners to also wear saris. Why not? There is a girl from Japan who is an avid Suta buyer, and she does all these dance reels to Bollywood songs in saris.

SB: I think somehow, the sari has become a garish attire. *Agar golden hai and studs hai toh bling,* wear it for a shaadi or Diwali. I am sure if foreigners realize how comfortable and beautiful a sari is, they will also want to wear it. The sari can be used to create twenty different looks from the same length of fabric just like baby wraps.

What is your typical day like?
SB: Everyone asks us how do you do all that you do. We live together on the same floor but in different apartments. Our kids are running

around, our dog is running around and our parents, who live with us, keep running after them. Our in-laws live close by. In the mornings, all of us work out, then we have breakfast together in Taniya's apartment. Afternoon is spent in my apartment. We then head to the office.

We make sure we have lunch with the family because that is one time that we give them that is fixed—we are not sure what time we will be back for dinner. After lunch, we can either attend office or work from home. Most days we wrap up work by 7:30 or 8 in the evening. Our days are packed with meetings or shoots or travel. We no longer need to travel to meet weavers; it is all done virtually though we try to meet them once or twice a year. The teams, whether it is the production team or the design, communicate with each other on a daily basis and everything runs smoothly. Travel is required for exhibitions, store openings and award ceremonies.

Could you tell us of the times when you had to face unexpected crisis and what you learnt from them? And other learnings from your journey.

TB: In 2017, our stall caught fire during The Lil Flea exhibition. It was horrible, we watched as our stock went up in flames.

SB: Taniya was sobbing and frozen from shock. And I was six months' pregnant.

TB: I was just standing and howling.

SB: The cash bag was lost in all the chaos and Taniya kept asking, 'How can this happen to us, how can this happen to us?'

TB: We had never thought we would find ourselves in a situation like that. Our stock was almost sold out, and on the last day we took all our inventory from the warehouse, which eventually got burnt at the exhibition. It was all the stock we had. Our saris were being trampled underfoot. For the next few days, we were just salvaging our saris.

Many people helped in different ways. After the fire was doused, some people helped us salvage something from the ashes and someone helped us find the cash bag, which had over two-and-a-half-lakh-of rupees. Someone located it, picked it up and handed it to us.

SB: The Lil Flea community contributed money for the burnt stock. We learnt about the power and the value of community that day and it stayed with us ever since. We also learnt that whatever happens in the night, you have to get up and show up in the morning. No matter what happens, you have to show up and things will fall in place.

TB: Also, we have learnt to never say no to anything. When an opportunity arrives, never turn it down. We also try to make sure we can help. We have also learnt over the years to ask for help. We are so guilty about everything. The guilt is overpowering. We are primary caregivers for everyone. It is okay to understand that we can't do everything perfectly. I keep telling everyone that I can't take care of my son, my mom does it.

SB: There was also the pandemic; when the lockdown was announced in March 2020, there were 10 of us stuck in a small three BHK. It was equally fun and terrible. Taniya was expecting then. We would walk from room to room. We did a lot of work in terms of fixing our website, fixing content, etc. Our list of weavers grew because they actively solicited work. Now that the brick-and-mortar stores were shut, they needed a source of income. They had stock lying with them that retailers were not picking up because everything was shut down. We picked their stock.

We announced online that we have not designed these but we are putting these up because we are helping weavers liquidate their stocks. And the response was very positive. Customers kept placing orders even while logistics were closed. When everything finally opened in October, we had 2,500 pending orders but only two people were allowed in the office at a time. We had decided we would not fire anyone through the lockdown even though the times were tough.

We were fortunate to hire the best talent at the time because even good people were getting fired then. There was no work. We spoke at a lot of webinars and college seminars. We told ourselves that if we don't give our 100 per cent right now, we will shut and nothing will happen. We decided to spread the light and that worked.

People admired our positivity and bought our saris, which confused us. Because people were stuck at home, no one was going out. So why buy our saris? People donned the attire even for their Zoom call meetings, which left us dazed. Some days we would lock ourselves in a room and cry. We were making sales and hence we could pay our workers. But there was no clarity as to what could happen in the days ahead. However, it all worked out well in the end.

SB: Another important lesson we learnt early is that it is important to create a support system for smooth running of one's day-to-day life. Additionally, we now understand the value of networking. In the past, I would feel uncomfortable approaching a group of men standing at a conference or function. I don't anymore. Instead I now walk up to them and say 'hi'.

TB: We have come to realize the value of building a team. As women, our natural instinct is to start doing everything ourselves. We tend to micromanage, and sometimes letting go is extremely difficult for women. So, we struggled initially, but we now have a fantastic team and we have learnt to let go, even though Suta is not just our business, it is our life.

13

"[F]or me, any kind of wealth feels pointless if I don't use it to help someone else achieve their dreams"

Vineeta Singh
Co-Founder and CEO,
SUGAR Cosmetics

If you asked Vineeta Singh, she would say she was the most unlikely person to start a cosmetics brand. She was never into cosmetics. She is a regular, professional woman, undoubtedly with magnificent bone structure, striking eyes and the model-like height that go well with the fashion and beauty business. On the day I met her, she had kohl and gloss and nothing beyond that. Cosmetics came into her life when she was sixteen, and that too the basics—only lip gloss and kajal.

It is interesting then, that she would go on to become one of India's best-known and most-loved entrepreneurs in the beauty space as the CEO and co-founder of SUGAR Cosmetics, an outlier brand that launched first through the D2C route retailing purely online and via social media promotion, and is now a well-established homegrown cosmetics brand giving tough competition to multinational brands.

She has been a shark (that is, a judge/investor) on the business reality TV show *Shark Tank India* since the show started airing on

Sony Entertainment TV and SonyLIV back in 2021, called by some the most-loved judge on the show, thanks to her bringing her heart to her investment decisions. At the SUGAR Cosmetics head office in Powai, Mumbai, Vineeta sat behind a remarkably clear and uncluttered desk. A shelf placed discreetly at the side of the rather simple cabin displayed the awards she had won. She was dressed in her favourite bright hues—fuchsia and red—functional trousers and a shirt with sneakers, telling us that she was not a woman who believed in either blending in or staying still.

She is an unlikely entrepreneur. If anything, it would have seemed that the young Vineeta Singh would have gone into the medical field or into academia given that her parents were both highly qualified researchers and academicians. She grew up on the AIIMS campus in Delhi, where her father, Dr Tej Pal Singh, a biophysicist, was determined to compile the largest number of protein structures in the world, and her mother, Dr Meera Singh, a PhD, worked at the Indian Council of Medical Research. She studied at Delhi Public School, R.K. Puram, then went on to IIT Madras and IIM Ahmedabad (IIMA) for her degree in electrical engineering in 2005 and her MBA in 2007, respectively.

The kernel of the idea of entrepreneurship came to her when she providentially was on the same flight as her to-be head of department at IIT Madras while flying to Chennai to join the institute. He was the one who after chatting with her for a while, put the idea of entrepreneurship into her mind. Till then, Vineeta had no clue about entrepreneurship as a possible career option.

She started off on her journey of becoming an entrepreneur right after completing her MBA in a radical departure from what was the expected norm for one who had passed out from the MBA program. While at IIM Ahmedabad, she had interned with Deutsche Bank, and was offered a starting salary of Rs 1 crore to join up, an offer she declined, much to the shock of everyone around her. She was clear; she was determined to give entrepreneurship a shot. "If not now, then when?" she told herself. Her parents were shocked as were her batchmates and professors.

It was unthinkable that someone would give up a salary that huge to risk the uncertainty of entrepreneurship. But Vineeta was clear, she had no student loan, no liability, this was the best time for her to take the leap of faith.

She was barely 23 at the time, young and raring to make her stamp in the world as an entrepreneur; becoming yet another corporate professional was not something that interested her. She and another graduate from the same batch had plans to start a lingerie business. Her refusal to take the offer from Deutsche Bank made her a star of sorts—the youngest at the time to receive a Rs 1 crore offer, and then refuse it—with interviews and newspaper articles featuring her. The lingerie business unfortunately did not find any funders, and she had to scrap the idea. In 2007, she started her first company, Quetzal, which was a B2B (business-to-business) company providing background verification checks to recruiters.

She put in the years and the slog, but the company went nowhere. She took the hard call to close down and begin something completely new, and so began FAB BAG in 2012, along with her husband, Kaushik Mukherjee, a subscription-based beauty product B2C (business-to-consumer) offering, which was closer to her heart, but after a few years of sustained effort, it became clear that this too was not destined to succeed as it should.

At this point, most people would give up, and consider joining the corporate world with a secure monthly salary and all the perks that come with it. But not Vineeta. Even in her darkest moments, she was sure that she was not going to give up on entrepreneurship. She then pivoted the business into a cosmetics brand, SUGAR Cosmetics, in 2015.

The couple had met during their stint at IIMA as MBA students and eventually got married. They brought to the table their complementary skills while Vineeta brought in domain/consumer knowledge and sourcing expertise, Kaushik's background as an internet entrepreneur helped set up the online business across direct to consumer (D2C) and other online marketplaces.

SUGAR Cosmetics, a D2C venture, became very popular with young women, targeting as it did regular young working women with diverse skin tones and textures, while offering the promise of easy application and long-lasting benefits. She drew her inspiration from the over 200,000 women who had been giving them feedback on the products that worked for them from FAB BAG and knew exactly what consumers were looking for.

The Indian consumer, they found, wanted colour cosmetics that would work with their skin tones, would last through an entire working day, and withstand heat and humidity. Initially, though, they came up against a wall with funding. They had Rs 30 lakh left as their working capital in the bank when everyone they spoke to advised them that it would take nearly Rs 50 crore or more to build a brand via advertising and marketing, with television budgets being what they were!

They cut costs, retrenched staff, cut down warehouse sizes to half and tightened their belts as much as they possibly could. They met over 100 investors, who told them it would not work. The market was too cluttered and Indian women used far fewer cosmetics when compared with women in the West or even South East Asia. It was disheartening, but they persevered.

Vineeta knew that she had figured out something important for the Indian cosmetic consumer and she was clear about how she was going to address that need with her products. She sourced her first lip crayons from Germany with a Rs 1 crore personal loan from an investor and soon there was no looking back.

In 2022, she closed a $50-million deal with private equity firm L Catterton, and in September of the same year, Bollywood actor Ranveer Singh invested an undisclosed amount, even becoming a brand evangelist for SUGAR Cosmetics. SUGAR Cosmetics was on a roll, and the milestones, Rs 100 crore, Rs 200 crore, kept coming in. In its Series D round in 2022, the company raised substantial funding, taking its capital to $85.5 million. The brand, which began its journey with a seed fund of just Rs 1 crore, saw its top line grow by 75 per cent to Rs 222 crore in FY22. Since opening its first offline store in 2019, SUGAR has expanded its footprint to over 100 exclusive brand outlets and is now present in more than 50,000 retail touchpoints across India.

The brand has also made a strong digital mark, with over 7 million app downloads and a leading presence on Instagram, where it holds the distinction of being India's number one consumer brand. Today, SUGAR offers a diverse portfolio of over 550 products catering to customers across metros as well as Tier II and III towns. With an offline-to-online revenue split of approximately 60:40, the company continues to strengthen its retail presence while exploring growth opportunities in international markets like the US, Russia, Gulf Cooperation Council (GCC) countries and Nepal.

Vineeta's aim at SUGAR Cosmetics is clear, she wants to build a brand for women by women, and have 75 per cent women as part of the company. She hopes to eventually get to hiring 10,000 women at SUGAR Cosmetics. She has received a number of accolades and she wears them lightly. In 2021, *Forbes India* listed her in the W-Power list of women achievers. In the same year, she was named in the Business World Disrupt 40 Under 40 awards. She was included in the GQ Most Influential Young Indians 2023, IMPACT 50 Most Influential Women List 2023, as well as Fortune's 40 Under 40. She made it to the World Economic Forum's Young Global Leadership list in 2022.

In 2024, she was named CEO of the Year at the SABRE Awards, and in 2025, she was recognized as Elle's Business Icon of the Year. These are not achievements she sought, as she says, she just kept building, keeping her nose to the grindstone and working at it.

While work is demanding, and building an Indian cosmetic brand she aspires to take to the world can be intensely stressful, she unwinds by running. A triathlete and ultramarathon runner, she has participated in over 20 marathons and over a dozen half marathons. She has to her credit the 89-kilometre Comrades Marathon and the 2017 Ironman Triathlon in Austria. Nothing stops her, not pregnancy, not motherhood, not building businesses.

In fact, she even ran 21 kilometres at the 2018 Mumbai Marathon while she was six months' pregnant, and finished her first triathlon carrying her then 11-month-old son. Unstoppable? She darned well is, and Vineeta Singh and SUGAR Cosmetics are set to go places no

Indian cosmetic brand has gone to hitherto. We can only watch and cheer from the sidelines.

Excerpts from our interview conducted in October 2023:

Tell us a bit about your childhood, your family, growing up on the AIIMS campus, and any anecdotes if you remember that impacted you perhaps and sowed the seed of entrepreneurship in your mind, if at all.

My dad actually came from poverty to get a job at AIIMS. He had lost both his parents before he turned five and had a very deprived childhood. By just working hard and studying well, he went to Indian Institute of Science (IISc) and then finally ended up getting a job at AIIMS. So, for him the road to having a decent life had been through education.

My mother grew up in a Gujarati household where there was never any expectation for women to be highly educated and make a career for themselves, so she was never expected to study much. Nonetheless, her mother was keen that she should pursue her higher education. She earned her PhD and then worked all her life at the Indian Council of Medical Research right next to AIIMS.

So, both of them always saw education as the means to self-respect, dignity, all those things that they did not always have. I was always told that if I had to have financial freedom, if I wanted to have self-respect in whatever I do in life, education is super important. Also, Dad has always been super ambitious; he was a topper at IISc, and before that he had topped at Allahabad University also.

Today he is 74 and we do not live on the AIIMS campus any more because we are technically not AIIMS staff any more, but he still travels 45 minutes one way every day to his lab at the AIIMS campus because he is still working on these protein structures. He is now the highest contributor in the world on protein structures. He crossed that milestone at the age of 71, and it has taken him 41 years to get there—probably because he has always been very ambitious.

I am an only child, so all of that aspiration, ambition and pressure, call it what you may, fell on me. So, I remember, I was in eighth grade and my mother had gone for some WHO work to the US, and Dad and I were by ourselves for six months, and I remember, every fourth night he would take me for ice cream opposite the IIT Delhi gate and tell me that someday I will be going there.

So, while growing up, I never really thought I had any option but to do extremely well academically. At that time it was because my parents wanted me to do this. I did not personally have an ambition as a child to grow up and be somebody who is great at what she does, as well as has a family, etc. I never had the imagination of what I would be in the future.

I never personally had any 'best-in-the-world' kind of ambitions. Both my parents were working, so when they were away I would steal some time to watch television without them knowing and chat for hours with my friends. My parents did not put in a cable connection for the longest time, and Doordarshan had limited options for kids. They just kept motivating me, so I did not know what I wanted to be but I knew that I did not want to be a doctor. Since we were living on the AIIMS campus, all my friends' parents were doctors, and I just thought that their life was so hard because everybody was on call 24 hours.

You had a good place to stay and had job safety as AIIMS was a great brand to be associated with. There was a lot of respect for that profession. But I was clear that I did not want to be a doctor. I saw Dad work seven days a week in his lab, and he had a clear aspiration of crossing 600 protein structures, and he was adding not even 15 a year, so it was like a senseless goal which seemed absolutely irrational to me. He was not able to make time for any of our family events, so I started wondering what sense did this make?

Dad had seen in his lab that a lot of women at some point lose their drive. He would come back and tell me a lot of stories of exceptionally talented women who would work in his lab and when they got married, they lost interest in the job.

So, it was one of his pet peeves, so to speak—why women were not as focused on their careers. It was not only pressure on me, but everybody. My extended family from Dad's side, and Mom's side, the women would fear coming over because they would get lectured on how they were not focused on their careers. Someone was getting married and was naturally very excited about it. She came over with her wedding invite, and Dad would go, 'Yes, yes, but what about your career?' Folks would be terrified coming home because Professor Singh would give them a huge lecture about not giving up their careers.

This was in the 1990s. He would go to extreme measures. My mom and my grandmom would make the best food ever, my grandmom would make the finest of rotis, *dhoklas,* etc., and they were amazing. Dad would actively discourage me from learning anything of that. He would be like do you want to be the best in the world in your career or do you want to make the thinnest roti ever? He would come up with the most ridiculous extreme statements like that which at that time made no sense to me because I thought that my dad was making me a unidimensional person who didn't know anything else in life.

But, I realize in hindsight, he was over-indexing me on this whole career ambition thing because he realized that all the other exposure would take me to the other extreme.

The only two other women in my life were Mom and my grandmom, and they were great at cooking, they were always there for all the family events. So, I was raised more like my dad than my mom. I think that was my message from him. I didn't have to do any chores at home. When we had visitors at home, I wasn't expected to sit with them, I could say I had to study and go into my room. I didn't have the expectations of being a good cook or being social. The expectation from me was just to get good grades, and nothing else. For him, it was just to be present in your career and everything else will happen. I feel I was raised like a man because I didn't have any other expectations.

Later on, I struggled a lot with not knowing how to cook, for instance. A lot of the other skills I had to figure out when I started living by myself because I had everything taken care of for me at home. The message was clear that career is the only thing that matters, and it was an extreme message. At that time, the extremity would send me into rebellion. Like, at times I thought I should run away from home because there was so much pressure.

When I look back, I realize that all the social messages around me were so different—and the way I was being raised was very different from all my other girlfriends. The only other activity I did apart from studying was playing badminton. I was into sports. I didn't have much exposure to music, dancing, all of that. So, it just seemed a very different kind of childhood. It had a huge impact on what I want to be. I did end up getting a lot of Mom's genes luckily, where she is also somebody who is very much into family and social relationships.

I always knew I would put family matters first no matter what I do. And from Dad, I ended up getting unwittingly, that irrational passion: when you find something that you love doing, and you can dedicate your life to it, that can give you a lot more happiness than money ever can. That irrational passion for building something that takes 20 years, 30 years and staying with it, I think I got that from my dad, despite resisting it with all my might. My only thing was to not turn into somebody like my dad. I think all of us realize at some point how similar we are to our parents whom once we rebelled against.

When you were a young girl, what did you think you would be when you grew up? Did you see any women entrepreneurs around you? Who were your role models? How did the idea of entrepreneurship come to you? Was there an incident or a moment that triggered it? I first started thinking about entrepreneurship back during my IIT days, and I began reading all these books about entrepreneurs. At that time, Silicon Valley was becoming a thing. I had all these books on Richard Branson, Howard Schultz, Steve Jobs, Bill Gates. At that time, entrepreneurs in general and not just the family-business types, but first-generation entrepreneurs were so rare that you didn't even expect that you would find women.

So, when I read all those books it didn't feel like anything was missing. It was just that such few great people are entrepreneurs. The fact that I have read 20 stories on entrepreneurs and their lives and that all of them are men—it is something that I now think about and find astonishing in hindsight. So, there were no women entrepreneurs that I read of. I think the first woman entrepreneur that I got inspired by was Sarah Blakely, but that was in 2014 or 2015 when we read about her story of building Spanx. But till then there was nobody.

But this sudden realization that there is no woman happened to me after my first business failed after five years. So, in 2007 I started my first company and by 2012 I finally got out of it. That was the lowest point in my life when I realized I had failed after giving five years of my life, and despite a lot of effort, it had amounted to nothing. I got nothing out of it—peanuts! At that time, the biggest self-doubt I had was that perhaps I wasn't meant to be an entrepreneur. And that's when the pattern started hitting me, all of these people had one thing in common: they were men.

They are these incredible, genius, visionaries; they have this alpha way of motivating tons of people to believe in their dream, their vision and to follow them, etc., and that is what it takes and that they are these genius salespeople who have managed to sway investors into giving them billions of dollars, which they use to build great technology, and I thought that I am so not like them. I am very honest about things. When I speak about numbers, I'll give very realistic numbers rather than provide lofty predictions.

I never saw myself as a visionary genius. I always saw that my greatest quality is my work, passion, empathy and being transparent. But does that matter in becoming an entrepreneur? Maybe not. That was when it started hitting me in 2012, that this pattern fitted a gender and there was probably nobody to show that it could be done without these. And I remember that phase for me was very hard, I wondered if I had made the right decision, but I realized that all the other options for me had then closed and I didn't have any option to go back to a good job. I mean, who would hire someone who is a failed entrepreneur?

Even if someone hired me, I would probably get Rs 50,000, which was nothing compared to the massive compensation that I had rejected five years ago. And that was when I think I sort of decided that I was going to go back in and try something else, maybe a different kind of business. And I realized that there are certain businesses that founders are meant to do. I felt that a consumer-facing business was a better fit for me, my previous business was a B2B which involved sales to large corporations. It was just tremendously hard because you had to network and I hated all of that.

And while that had seemed like a drudgery, this seemed like a lot of fun. I restarted but with very different kinds of expectations, just saying, let's see where this goes. I began readjusting myself. I read all the books, and then I thought I couldn't be like them. This was not possible for me. I don't know if I made the right choice, wrong choice whatever, but I didn't have any other option. So, I said I am going to give this another four, five, ten years and I am going to try something different. I am not going to have these world-domination plans, I am going to do something that I enjoy doing. And that is how FAB BAG came into being.

Growing up, it was such a different kind of upbringing on the AIIMS campus. I remember that there was one vacation, when my best friend and I were 12 years old, and we created a magazine called *Kid's Corner*. We wrote stories, drew illustrations, sort of created with pen on paper, and then xeroxed copies in Dad's lab and stapled them, going door to door to sell them at Rs 3 thinking that it is what anyone would blindly pay. And of the 70–80 households, three people bought copies and it was such a disaster that we came back with all the copies.

When I look back now, I realize that all those things were entrepreneurial in their own way—you did something and learned lessons about rejection, selling, and so on. But because the word entrepreneurship had never been used back then in one's life, it just seemed like a normal thing to do. I never saw any of the other experiences I had as a kid as signalling anything around entrepreneurship. Much later, around four or five years ago, when I turned 35, I doubted whether I was meant to be an entrepreneur. Or was it all a bet gone wrong?

You rejected a job offer from Deutsche Bank with a package of Rs 1 crore to venture into entrepreneurship. When that didn't take off, how did you bring yourself back from the dejection and start again? Did you ever feel like you took a wrong decision at that point? First, I will tell you how this entire entrepreneurship thing began. When you grow up in Delhi, even if you grow up in the relative safety of the AIIMS campus, there is so much fear. Your parents are always afraid, your freedom ends up being curbed by yourself and your parents because it just did not feel safe. So, I always thought that I was going to get out of Delhi and live in a hostel, figure out life by myself, away from any family pressures, etc. And so, when I got through IIT, although I had the option of going to IIT Delhi, I decided to go to IIT Madras.

I convinced my parents that I always wanted to do electrical engineering, and not mechanical engineering, because I was getting mechanical engineering in IIT Delhi which was barely five kilometres from my house. I was very clear that I was not going to give up four more years of freedom, and I had to go as far away as possible, so I went to Chennai. Everyone had told me that IIT Madras had the scariest electrical engineering HOD, he was like Hitler, he flunked everyone, etc. And on my first flight, as we were taking off, I was sitting on the flight, reading my best friend's letter and crying and I heard someone's voice behind me saying, 'I teach at IIT Madras.'

I thought, *Oh my God, there is someone I will know.* Because I knew no one in Chennai apart from this person whose notes I got. So, I swapped seats with the person next to the person who said he was teaching at IIT Madras and introduced myself, saying, 'I am going to be studying electrical engineering.' And then he takes out his card; it said 'Prof. Jhunjhunwala' Head of Department, Electrical Engineering. I replied, 'I've heard so much about you.'

Then to my regret, I realized that the Delhi–Chennai flight is two hours forty-five minutes. It started off with him asking me about the difference between digital and analogue, how a transistor works and all these questions to which I had no answer. Then he asked me, 'What do you want to do in life?'

I gave him some kind of gibberish saying that I wanted to work in an organization where I could contribute. He interrupted me and asked, 'Tell me what will really make you happy?' I pondered a lot about it and then replied, 'I think being rich.' And then, he said, 'Based on all the conversation we've had so far, I really feel that while you've taken engineering, that's not something you'll really be passionate about. I really think you should seriously consider entrepreneurship, if you do something well, the money comes, but that's something that you would enjoy building.'

He just dropped this word, entrepreneurship, at that moment. From engineering school, nobody ever became an entrepreneur. Everyone who graduated from IIT would apply to a US university for an M.S.

and go there, by default. And I was so struck by what he said, and it sort of made sense. I had taken electrical engineering as a parachute of sorts to have some freedom and I knew this was not going to take me to the right place and I was looking for another thing where all of this starts making sense. And suddenly there was this word, I didn't even know what it meant, but I told myself I am going to explore this.

For four years I read up on every biography and followed up on what was happening in tech in the US. Basically, I graduated from IIT having the conviction that someday I was going to be an entrepreneur, but I did not know when or how. Someone told me that IIM Ahmedabad has a course on entrepreneurship, so I studied to get into IIMA, and I wanted to take that course but that year, the professor decided that he was not going to take that course. So, I showed up at his place and told him, 'I came here to do this course. I want to figure out entrepreneurship because nobody is becoming an entrepreneur. But I feel this is something that is going to happen. In the US, people are leaving engineering schools and going to business schools to become entrepreneurs. This is going to happen in India, and I need that inspiration to be trained and mentored in entrepreneurship.' He agreed to mentor me. This was Professor Sunil Handa, who became my mentor and he kept telling me, 'If you decide to take up a job what is it that you will learn? You will be but one cog in the wheel of a large company. How will you learn how to start a business? The only way to learn how to start a business is to start a business. Why not start just right away?'

Because I had this investment banking offer, I really thought a lot about it. I even went and did an internship to understand what it is like to be a banker and I came back with extreme clarity. I realized I didn't want to settle in the UK or anywhere else. I want to build and I want to build in India. Probably, it was going to be super hard, but just like in the US there was going to be a wave coming and it will get easier. And the earlier I get on this wave and revolution, the better my learnings from this will be, so why wait for later?

Thanks to my parents who paid for my education, I did not have an education loan. I thought to myself, *I don't have a loan, I don't have any liabilities, let me start up.* It was extreme optimism because till that point, I never really failed, I always thought that life was easy and rosy, and so I thought *I was going to build this business up.* And my parents would often ask, 'Why would you put everything you worked so hard for at stake?' I told them, 'Don't worry, give me two years, in two years I'll show you how it makes sense, and if in two years it doesn't make sense I'll go back to the corporate world.'

Two years later, it was all a disaster, and I told them to give me two more years and at the end of five years when nothing worked, I was at my lowest point. I remember telling my parents, 'Yes you were right' and they said, 'As long as you're enjoying what you are doing, it's fine'. The biggest worry they had about me was *shaadi hogi ki nahin hogi* (Will I get married or not?). But by then, I was married.

What I thought would be a two-year, three-year, four-year, five-year gamble, turned out to be the gamble of my entire life. I learned that nothing happens in two years, three years, four years, or five years and it takes you very long to figure that out. But the more you keep building, the more you get excited about the idea of building. Then even if there is no result, you are inspired to show up every day at work, you try new things, you are failing, it is a fun ride. I started enjoying that rollercoaster.

While I probably left that job offer thinking I was going to make a lot more money, I didn't for the longest time, that is, almost 15–16 years. I couldn't even pay myself that much, and by the time things came around, and not the two to five years that I had imagined when I first started. I at least have the satisfaction now that I wrote my own pay cheque. And now I get to write the pay cheque of 4,000+ other people, including 3,000+ other women. These are a few things that I didn't think about when I decided to become an entrepreneur.

Honestly, I just thought about making money, doing something in a short period, not being like my dad and all those things. But none of that happened, but that was life which had other plans. Luckily, that worked out for me. The more you chase money, the more it doesn't happen, but when you just love what you are doing, it comes around. When you keep working on a problem for a long period, it builds and you make money too. I have so many friends I speak with who often say, ' By 40 I'll make so much money, and then I'll do what I love', and I tell them that never happens. Instead, if you invert it, and you say I will do what I love from day one then you can end up working 50 years or so.

When you are 23, you feel 50 years is so long. But now I have seen Dad who has put 50 years of his life into discovering protein structures. I am not like Steve Jobs, I am not like those male entrepreneurs, I don't have that charisma, that genius, maybe I can't do it in two years, three years, but maybe I can do it in 15 years, 20 years. I can create something completely different, and that was when I understood that entrepreneurs come in all shapes, sizes and genders and it helps if you have that genius but even if you don't, you show up every single day. You are transparent with your team, you get a set of smart people together, empower them and create something that you love working towards. You can come together and build something which is of amazing value. That is what entrepreneurship is. It is not a race where only the biggest valuation or somebody who gets it in the shortest time wins. I might not get there the fastest, but I will surely get there.

You set up a couple of ventures before SUGAR Cosmetics finally took off. What made you choose those very different spaces, Quetzal and FAB BAG? What were your learnings from both, and is it important for an entrepreneur to experience failure to finally make it?
With our enterprise company, Quetzal, there was a massive learning around sales, which was that as an entrepreneur, your most important job has to be sales. Growing up always doing well in class, and as somebody who is focused on just studies, the whole idea of how to sell was alien and that is something they don't teach you at B-school. You learn how to sell by selling something.

Money is something that doesn't get discussed in Indian families, selling involves money so it looks cheap, right? But on the first day of my first business, it occurred to me that to pay people's salaries you need revenue and to get revenue you have to sell. So, I was literally on the road, 20 days a month, meeting customers, trying to get business and I learned so much about selling.

I learned that just like everything else you just have to keep doing it to get more confident at it. The greatest fear we have is of getting rejected, and I have a lot of fear. I used to do these cold calls, and on every single call, I would feel like somebody was going to punch me from the other side of the phone. I used to shiver and try to get the courage. I would do around 90 cold calls in a day and it used to be super stressful. The more I did it, the more it occurred to me that it was one of the things I was afraid to do, but the only way I could overcome it was by doing it.

Also, I realized later that there is a very big thing called the founder market fit. You have that one thing in you that you want to do. I feel every entrepreneur has that one thing in them that they want to build something. For me, I think that thing is building something for women, where a woman is at the heart of the consumption. It was only when I had that eureka moment that I realized I was climbing the wrong tree because I was not finding my *ikigai*. FAB BAG started as a beauty subscription company where every month you could get four to five products curated as per the algorithm. We went up to about Rs 7–8 crore in revenue.

We were not profitable and we had to pivot out of it because we realized that for every additional customer, the customer would make us lose money. We spent so much on acquiring the customer, and explaining to her what the service is, so it was an idea far ahead of its time in terms of subscription. Anyways, India is not a market where subscriptions are going to work because people don't trust you with so much money in advance. The other thing I learned was that sometimes we overcomplicate things in our effort to be different.

If I started a makeup business, everyone would say that there are a thousand brands, what is so different about this one? In that effort to find differentiation, sometimes you complicate things so much that your consumer does not understand it. So you might say we have an algorithm to curate products and have a monthly subscription. But what does it mean to the customer?

I remember in the FAB BAG journey, there were so many times we got the feedback from the consumers that could we just get a single product and buy it, rather than getting the whole bag and signing up for the whole subscription. But there were so many brands doing this and we were so focused on the curated subscription bag that we weren't seeing the opportunity.

When our backs were against the wall, we realized that to add every single lakh of revenue, we would have to burn money. It stopped making sense. And that time there was the option to shut this down and build something else from scratch. Kaushik and I had a long conversation and contemplated whether one of us should get back to a job because both of us had put all our eggs in this basket.

He had mentioned a couple of times, 'Let me just drop this and pick up a job.' A brand business is a traditional one where there is no role of technology and it is not going to be purely e-commerce, so what is the point if it is not going to be large enough to sustain both of us.

At that point, I was thinking that we have come so far and there is so much feedback that we have got from our women. Our consumers were these young women who were telling us over and over again that the three to four products that you are sending us, in that the one makeup product does not last long enough, it is not value for money and this is the most important product for them.

So, whether the bag was a make or a break depended on the makeup product's quality. They had feedback on how we could do it better.

SUGAR Cosmetics came from this consumer feedback where we realized that traditional brands didn't get young women. They made products for women who were not working and the only time they wore makeup was when they went for a shaadi or a function, so the products they created were meant to last for two to three hours. But this new consumer is a girl who is going to college, who is working and she needs a product that lasts from 9 a.m. to 8 p.m., and that was a different kind of product. That was the first realization.

The second was that a lot of these girls were now beginning to have access to smartphones and social media, and what a lot of traditional brands thought was that e-commerce was going to be like a discounting dump yard and it is not going to be where brands are built. They never expected that Indian women would apply lipstick and tag the brand on Instagram.

They thought it would all be driven by television advertising and digital would be just an extension of television advertising. They didn't expect it to become so huge and so user-generated, so to speak. But we got all of that because at FAB BAG we were so close to the consumer that every month we got a ton of bouquets and brickbats where they would say I hate this, I love this, and segregating all of that sort of got us to SUGAR Cosmetics.

But till we were at the stage where we had a team of 30 who were with FAB BAG, it was very hard because your money comes from the business which you are now not willing to bet on. You have to turn the tap off there and switch to something new. This also means you have to extend your runway because nobody is going to fund you for the next two years so you have to make sure that you make that money last, and we had only about Rs 30 lakh in the bank. And so, we cut the team from 30 to some 15 people, we cut our office into half, cut our warehouse into half.

We spoke to the team and told them that unfortunately, we won't be able to have any increments for the next two years or so, it was an experiment we were trying. But pivots are lonely. It is you on your own and you don't know whether it will work or not, you have to slowly taper it out while building something new. That part was super tough, but somehow Kaushik and I agreed on building SUGAR Cosmetics together because we felt that there was going to be enough opportunity in India. We were beginning to think that maybe people would stop frowning at the idea of 'made in India' for makeup brands and start giving Indian brands a chance. Maybe the internet and social media will grow faster than what we expect, and whether that happens or not it does not matter, there are these young women who will love what we are offering. We understood that consumer very well.

So, SUGAR Cosmetics started with a small dream—we will create a makeup brand that will satisfy young women so that they find products they love so much that they tell their friends and share about them on social media, and we would not need to spend anything on marketing.

We launched with just four colours of our crayon lipsticks, one eyeliner and one kajal, and they were super long-lasting. We put a lot of effort into getting the four shades right for the Indian skin tone such as the right shade of red, nudes, pink and berry. It emerged that women wanted a nude lipstick but one that would work for deeper skin tones. In 2015 December, we launched lipstick crayons which began going viral.

We still struggled a lot for two years for money because working capital was very hard, we had to borrow from our parents and investors, who had already invested, and who gave their money from personal savings. But by then we were seeing traction and we were seeing love. The difference between a FAB BAG and SUGAR Cosmetics was that in FAB BAG we were convincing people to buy something whereas in

SUGAR Cosmetics they were coming back for more and more, and we were struggling to keep things in stock.

So, by default, it began taking off, and the Rs 100-crore and Rs 200-crore milestones came, I think the signs were clear. Young women loved the brand. Can we go beyond just young women? Can we go beyond just the internet? All those questions we went through. That was when we started, from 2012 to 2017, seeing this was it, thinking it has got to be big.

Why the name SUGAR Cosmetics?

So, the name SUGAR Cosmetics was something that Kaushik actually came up with. The honest story is that the name that Kaushik and I had first come up with was Kickass. The idea was that we were going to make a brand for young women, a young and rebellious brand, so 'kickass' was a term we associated with unstoppable women. We were excited about it. We even registered the domain name. We went to a bunch of investors and said this is the name we have and they said *thoda consumer research kar lo;* in other words, speak to a few women. So, we spoke to 40–50 women.

We gave them four to five alternatives to Kickass, one of the alternatives was SUGAR, one was Pepper, one was Fabulicious and there was Stoked. We created this nice Instagram kind of imagery around each name, we presented it and asked them to share their thoughts on it. We then realized that Kickass was such a bad name, and the clear winner was SUGAR Cosmetics because so many women said they felt like they had heard of the brand before, they associated with it, it was this fun simple name that was so relatable.

And yes, of course, now I joke about it that SUGAR Cosmetics gives you the sugar rush without the calories, but that was not the first name. It was just a lucky stroke that we ended up having SUGAR Cosmetics as an option and went with it.

Were you a beauty product fan before you got into FAB BAG and then SUGAR Cosmetics? How did you spot the opportunity in this space, which was so dominated by the big brands? What was the differentiator for SUGAR Cosmetics according to you?

I was somebody who was the typical engineer. My mom, by the way, does not even have her ears pierced, or wear jewellery. So, we grew up with no jewellery, no makeup at home. Amongst my dad's many quirks, one was that putting metal on your body does not make sense, so I actually pierced my ears after my 12th boards. I figured kajal, lip balm and all of that from my friends, so I really was not a makeup expert. My excitement over getting into this space came from my desire to build something for women. I just felt that this was the one demographic that was really going to change. Nobody was going to get the change except for a woman. I thought a woman had to create that. Then, of course, FAB BAG happened and I started playing around a lot more with makeup and I got really comfortable with it.

Many a time when I am sitting in the lab with my team I have asked the dumbest questions, just like any average Indian girl would. I don't have flawless skin that makes everything appear amazing on me. Making makeup for normal skin types and making them appear fantastic is more important than making it for flawless skin. I think I speak for the average Indian girl who wants to use makeup but is hesitant about applying, and has these very basic questions about it.

She wants products that are super easy to use, is not an expert and does not see herself as an expert. That, I feel, helps me create products that are relatable to the girl next door. More and more brands need to create products for everyday women. You can only do that when you relate to the consumer. While it can be perceived as my greatest weakness that I came into the business without having played with makeup for 25 years, as many women do, I feel I made it my greatest strength by asking more and more questions and making it easier and easier to use.

For instance, we are the only brand that has this, our bestselling product, a foundation stick that sells for Rs 1099, which is expensive compared to the normal, a very matte long-lasting foundation that comes with a brush at the other end. Because from my experience and after speaking with many women, I realized that more than half of the users don't have a beauty blender or a brush at home. They use their fingertips and when you use a matte foundation with your fingers, it does not blend. Just having a high-quality brush made it easy for them to get the kind of coverage they wanted. What a lot of women would do is buy foundation and never use it because they feared it would look cakey.

This made it easier for them not to be afraid. So, the question I am always asking is how do you make sure it does not lie untouched on her shelf and that she picks it up and uses it? How do you ensure that it is easy for her and not make her embarrassed or feel that people will judge her for having a lot of make-up? These are things that Indian women are dealing with. There are certain preconceived notions around makeup—that it is associated with educated women, that women who are from certain families don't wear makeup and people who are not North Indian don't wear makeup. You know, there are all of these types of deeply ingrained beliefs that women around deal with when it comes to makeup.

So, when you wear lipstick to work, you are fighting some of those, right? I just try to make it easier for them. I just believe that being a regular working woman made it easier for me to understand the consumer, as against coming from a place where it is normal to wear makeup. For instance, you should know how to wing an eyeliner and I am always the first person asking how we can make it simpler, how we can take this trend and dumb it down so much so that somebody does not feel that she is going to have to spend 40 minutes struggling to apply it.

How easy or difficult is it to partner with your spouse? What are the skills you both bring to the table, and how have you managed to demarcate work responsibilities without stepping on each other's toes?

We struggled a lot. I think every time somebody attempts this there should be a lot of disclaimers. You have to take a couple of years to figure it out, and for us those couple of years were very ugly, having arguments at the office, carrying them home, not speaking to each other for days. We went through all of that. But I think there were two-three things that worked for us.

Firstly, we had clear demarcations on who does what, with no stepping on each other's toes. Each person had veto power in their area. So, we have so many disagreements, but it is defined. If something that is related to retail or product, my say is final. If it is something related to marketing or finance, Kaushik's decision is final. So, we express our dissatisfaction, hear each other's views but the person in charge takes the final call and has the responsibility of making that work. And that is important not just for founder couples, I think, but for any co-founders. At the end of the day there will be a decision which is not great, everything cannot come from data. So, you have to be able to disagree and figure out a way to work together despite all this, and have the dignity to not say 'I told you so',—that it makes it harder for people to make decisions.

Secondly, I think the one big thing was clearly defined roles, staying in our own lanes and knowing that the decision will be taken by the one responsible. I think it just generally reminded ourselves why we started in the first place. I think that as couples and co-founders, that trust and respect can be tremendously high, but sometimes you tend to take it for granted, and that is when you sort of lose track and ego comes in the way. I feel that the most important thing for any partnership to work is leaving ego at the door. Again, not trying to do what is right, but trying to do what is in the best interests of the family and the business. You get used to taking those decisions, and you get used to realizing that trying to be right doesn't help.

Thirdly, we have miserably failed in trying to not discuss shop at home or vice versa. We have two children and both have demands, and it is difficult to demarcate home and work. For instance, you have a work trip and you will ask the other to step in when it comes to school duties, or pick up, or meet the teacher. Many times, there are dinner-table conversations, where my son will suddenly say, 'Okay, stop talking business now.'

We have a store in Powai, near our home. My little one has picked up phrases like 'today there were two customers in the store, so finally footfall is back'. Because they hear us talk about it over and over. So yes, you need to be able to draw the line and not get personal in business and all that but we have absolutely failed at that, we are discussing work all the time. The good thing is that we never run out of things to talk about, whether it is about the competition or the investors— that also brings us together.

You must have definitely encountered sexism at play in your journey. Funding too was conditional on bringing in a male co-founder. Could you tell us about this and other such incidents you may have experienced? And do you think things have changed for women entrepreneurs since you first started out?

For me, raising money was extremely hard. *Shark Tank* may make it look easy but it is really hard. The four biggest challenges include, first, that women-led companies globally get 2.6 per cent of global funding. In India, it is a lot worse, it is less than 2 per cent. The odds are not in your favour.

Second, at least until three or four years ago—though things have changed since—venture capitalists were not in favour of married couples as co-founders. Third, a women-led business was a big no-no. And the fourth, most importantly, was that 99 per cent of the VCs are men. For them, to understand the business that does not serve an obvious need of women was hard. I really used to find it hard to convince VCs that women care a lot that lipstick lasts for eight hours versus two hours. That concept was not very obvious to them. Because there are fewer women running businesses and solving problems for other women, those kinds of businesses will get funded much less than those which serve the needs of everyone.

Ours was a very women-centric business. So, for us, it was very, very hard. When we started FAB BAG, Kaushik was still working with McKinsey for about six to eight months. I did about 70 to 80 VC pitches, and got rejected by every single one of them. There was only one best-case scenario, which was that we could invest only if Kaushik came on board full time.

In 2012, it was so rare for women-founded companies to get funded that it was not even considered sexist to say these kinds of things— like I remember, I was told by a VC that I invested in this woman-led company and she got married and decided to have a family, and stopped focusing on the company and my funding went nowhere. And I would say yes, but your sample size is one, and once you build it enough you will know whether it is a pattern or an aberration. At that time, you couldn't really call out these things.

I remember I used to have conversations with Kaushik, this is what the investor said, and anyway, if that is what it takes to get the money, let's take the money. One could be all feminist about it and say I'm going to call this out, but if one felt there was some way of getting the money might as well do that because there was no one else willing to come to the table.

Every single round, we had this joke—there is this IC round, which is the final round in a fundraising process, which is like a check in the box, no one gets rejected after that round. We were rejected twice in the IC rounds. I have had hundreds of rejections and they have been of all types. We were at a town hall where Kaushik pulled out these emails from all the VCs, including some which said things like 'you're a smart person, why are you doing this?' to politically correct responses. It was a hard journey. Now that I have sat in an investor's shoes, I can understand that some of that is not wrong because at the end of the day a VC's job is pattern matching—what were my successful companies, what did the founder look like, what did the market look like, does this fit that.

So, you are pattern matching because you do not have the ability to predict the future. But now when I think back, I realize that I can't blame them because they were pattern matching and we did not fit the pattern. It did not make sense for them and at the end of the day it is their job to do this. I now understand that all of those rejections came from a place of doing the right thing by all their investors, but for me it seemed like a very sexist and a very harsh world where it seemed impossible for a business like this to get funded. We would not have got the capital we got in the last three four years but luckily the business really took off.

Beyond that, there are these waves that come, so brands from India suddenly became this big VC theme in 2020–21 and we had not planned for that. We had started SUGAR Cosmetics five years before that but luckily, we were in the right place at the right time. Then suddenly, VCs were looking, and we had made a lot of progress, so in the last three to four years capital has been super easy for us and it has come from all sides. We did not have to look too much.

But I don't think we really had to do anything from our side apart from building our business, and not worrying about how much capital we were able to raise and the timing finally worked out for the best. So, I think if you stay at it and just build, sometime eventually you will get the timing right. And now I have seen so many cycles, and I realize everything happens in a cycle, as long as you keep building you should not really worry so much where the VCs are putting their money—you get lucky sometimes, at others you don't get lucky, it is all about a wave.

How did Shark Tank ***happen? As a judge on the show, have you taken back learnings and inspiration from the participants? What captures your attention during a pitch and what makes you back a business?***

As a kid, I used to believe a lot in karma. And then I would wonder how karma is not working, I am putting in so much of effort, and nothing is happening. Later on, I realized that it is not that you will put in effort and something like that will happen at that very moment. But if you work hard and keep doing things, good things happen. Some of it you did not even work for and still the good things happen. So, I think it all balances itself out, and I am a firm believer that if you play nice, work hard, be fair to everyone, good things will happen. I think *Shark Tank* was one of those things because I had not done a single personal investment, or angel investment until it happened. So, when they reached out to me, I thought it was a joke.

They reached out to Kaushik on Twitter and asked him to connect me with the Sony team. I met them, I auditioned with them. For the first two or three months, I thought I was not going to do this. I kept thinking where am I going to get so much liquidity from, where do I get so much bandwidth from? What happens when an entrepreneur who has a consumer brand goes on TV? Could there be a negative effect? All these questions were playing on my mind. I took a long time to make my decision, but Kaushik pushed me into it, saying, 'Come on, you have to start taking risks!'

So, I finally agreed to do it. It was one of those things when I got on to it, then I felt that I was playing above my level because everyone who came in had over 200 deals, were avid angel investors, and I was sitting there, not having done anything in my life. But, Season 1 happened, and it is one of those things that I feel so grateful for, I think it changed a lot for me. I meet so many six-, seven- and eight-year-old girls who come up to me and say, 'I want to become an entrepreneur' and their moms nod when they say that. I think that I never had that kind of role model who was a woman entrepreneur when I was growing up. At some point, it led me to the question of whether this is for me.

And these girls growing up would not have that question because they had seen me on television. For 10 weeks in a year they are seeing two or three women sitting there, one woman pitching, they are seeing women in the decision-making position, and they can see themselves, and that makes all the difference.

In the first season, I invested 50 per cent with companies that had a woman founder, in my second season it is around 60 per cent. I mean we are talking about 1–2 per cent in India, so suddenly *Shark Tank* gives you the ability to change the narrative. After that, other teams outside *Shark Tank* also have done so for women-led companies, and I feel that at least I have the ability to pay it forward, which for me is a huge deal. I mean financially, of course, being able to contribute to these women and their businesses but also emotionally. During COVID when they aired *Shark Tank* for the first time, so many businesses were on the brink of shutting down because it was a very tough year. So, I just thought that if they could see these stories and if they found the courage to continue for just one more day, one more month, sometimes that turning point comes.

I know, in our journey, 10 years, there was no turning point, no hope. But then suddenly, things take off and you become unstoppable. Every entrepreneur gets that moment in their journey where things finally start making sense. And the phase up to that point can be one year, two years, 10 years, 12 years, you can't predict. But if they are in there at that moment, their lives are going to change forever.

For me, it was a brilliant opportunity to have *Shark Tank* as a platform to showcase these stories. In Season 1, there was this company called Jhaji, these were two women who came from Darbhanga and they made *achar* (pickles). They were sisters-in-law, and in Season 1 they did not get funded. They were selling their yummy achars online. It was just that thought of whether they would be able to crack digital or not. Nobody invested.

After three to four months one of my batchmates reached out to me saying, 'One of these entrepreneurs called Jhaji, their numbers went up after *Shark Tank* and we have this Jharkhand Angels Network, and we are thinking of putting money in them, do you want to come in?' So, I called up Namita (Thapar), and both of us went to Darbhanga, saw their setup, their factory and invested in them. I saw the women they employed, saw the pride they were bringing to Darbhanga in building the business. It was something only they could do, make original Mithila achar. I don't know if it will become a Rs 500-crore business or not but it will be a good business. And *Shark Tank* allows you to be a part of such stories.

In the second season, at least 10 to 15 women participants told us that when they saw the Jhaji story, they told themselves that they would be there in the next season. There was this woman making laddoos, there was this woman making momos, making modaks. In India, if you know the number of self-employed women who are creating these things out of home, it is a large number and suddenly when they see somebody like them on television getting recognized, it is everything. Sometimes when I meet women, they are so excited—not just about me, but also about Namita and the other women who have brought inspiration to *Shark Tank*—that their hands are shaking as they click pictures with us.

I just feel that this is one of those things that I did nothing to be a part of. I was just doing my own thing, but this is one of those things that gives me a new dimension, a purpose to life and I feel very grateful to be part of it. Everybody told me it was going to fail; I had no idea it was going to be so huge. We thought who in India would watch conversations around money and investing at prime time. But people are watching, the grandparents, the parents, the kids. Across age groups. Sony TV knows their audience and they are making the programme in a way that does not come across as just business; it is business, plus inspiration, plus ideas, plus entrepreneurship. All of those stories, of so many people including women. In Season 1, 48 per cent of the pitchers were women. That was a lot compared with the actual start-up ecosystem.

Tell us about your running journey and how does Vineeta Singh unwind?

Just this morning I did an 8-km run. For me, running started as a crazy goal at IIMA. It was the third year of the Mumbai marathon which was basically a race where everyone who participated got a medal; was really a big event. So, we did not know that we had the option of choosing to run the half marathon therefore we signed up for the full marathon. We were a bunch of five or six of us on campus who would finish our classes and at one a.m., two a.m., go running on the streets of Ahmedabad.

The whole day was classes and project work, etc., so you would run in the night, come back, sleep for a couple of hours and then go to class at eight a.m. It was very hard, but I remember my first marathon in 2007—I had come down from Ahmedabad to Delhi, and after finishing it, I loved it. It felt like one of those things I would want to keep doing. I just felt free running. I used to play badminton as well for both my colleges and it was one of those things that I did as a passion, but the coordination involved in getting people together, getting a court in a city like Mumbai was proving to be tough. So, I decided, I was going to become a running person. It is something that helps me stay fit. I grew up on a hospital campus, so 'wealth is wealth' is something I learned later, but health is wealth is something I learned from Dad from the age of three or four. This thought was drilled into me, the need to keep fit and healthy. Even now, he walks some 15,000 or 20,000 steps a day apart from a full day's work. Mom also does two to three hours of yoga and various forms of exercise. She ran a half marathon at the age of 65, so they have always liked to stay fit and say if you want to enjoy your 70s and 80s, stay fit.

It was something that I thought running could give me. But more than that, the business has been so stressful and so hard for me, that running gave me some escape. Even in the worst of the 2012–13 phases, I started doing the ultramarathon and a few of the international races in South Africa and other places, where I ran some seemingly impossible distances and timings.

So, when everything else was going wrong in my life, this was the one thing that kept me going. Depression is a strong word, but I do feel that at that point, the only thing that kept my head held high was to feel that if I could really conquer races, I deserved all the education I had had, I deserved to build a great business. I feel that was a huge thing for me. Even now for me, it is very meditative, I go without my phone, no headphones, nothing. And I just go, and it is just me and my thoughts, so it is not meditation but it is as close to meditation as I can get.

If you do not have something like that in your life where you can go into a zone when you are running a stressful business, I think it is hard because all that stress accumulates in your body. You need a way to channel that stress and for me running is that. I just am a better person on the days that I run.

And finally, you have built SUGAR Cosmetics into a brand for women by women with a majority of your workforce being women. What next for SUGAR Cosmetics and Vineeta Singh?

For me, firstly, I feel strongly about building brands from India. I am going to continue to build and SUGAR Cosmetics is really at a great place to continue to become a global brand. I feel that there will be more brands and maybe SUGAR Cosmetics will go to more countries. That is something I feel proud of because I feel lucky to live in times when Indians are proud of buying Indian brands.

I have seen that journey from it being unthinkable to own a 'Made in India' product to being proud of it. Secondly, I feel equally strongly about making women's dreams come true—by employing over a thousand women, something I have often spoken about. One of the biggest impacts you want to make is that you come to this planet and want to make it a better place. The biggest impact that I can make is to create one of the best places to work for women.

Thirdly, thanks to this exposure I have had through *Shark Tank* and through the investments I have made, I want to continue making women entrepreneurs unstoppable because they are the ones solving our problems. The needs of Indian women are being addressed by these women entrepreneurs from smaller cities. I get a chance to be part of their journeys, I get a chance to help their dreams come true and for me, any kind of wealth feels pointless if I don't get to help someone else achieve their dreams. I am lucky that I have got the chance to do that.

Acknowledgements

Every book is a tapestry woven not just with words, but with the faith, labour and love of many who believed in it and worked on it. This book, in particular, is stitched together with the voices and visions of the women who dared to dream beyond boundaries.

I want to express my gratitude to Shantanu Ray Chaudhuri, chief editor of Om Books International, for believing in the idea of this book over a quick conversation, for taking this on without a moment's hesitation and for being its unstinting advocate.

A big thank you to my publisher Ajay Mago for standing behind this idea.

Much obliged to my editor Jyotsna Mehta for her incredible insights, extraordinary rigour and constant encouragement. You found the heartbeat of this book and ensured it never faltered.

Cheers to Sheena Agarwal for translating the spirit of these pages into an unapologetically beautiful and subtly profound cover.

To my literary agent, Suhail Mathur of The Book Bakers, I deeply appreciate your support through this book and the others over the years.

And to the fierce, phenomenal women who trusted me with their stories, this book belongs to you. Thank you for your candour, your grace, your fire, your resilience. Thank you for sharing the quiet phases of your journeys, the highs and the lows of striking out on your own, for sharing what has taken you so far. You have shown us—not told us—that it can be done, and all you need is dogged determination and unwavering faith in yourself, your abilities and what you are bringing to the world. It has been such an honour to listen, to learn and to bring your voices on paper.

Last but not least, this book is dedicated to all women who have persevered in building their lives, speaking truth and refusing to shrink. This book is also for every woman who refuses to contain her dreams within boxes that the world tries to fit her into. You are the revolution, boldly lived and written.